Prisoners of Our Past

Prisoners of Our Past

A Critical Look at Self-Defeating Attitudes Within the Black Community

by James Davison, Jr., Ph.D.

A BIRCH LANE PRESS BOOK
Published by Carol Publishing Group

A Birch Lane Press Book.
Published by Carol Publishing Group
Birch Lane Press is a registered trademark of Carol Communications, Inc.
Editorial Offices: 600 Madison Avenue, New York, N.Y. 10022
Sales and Distribution Offices: 120 Enterprise Avenue, Secaucus, N.J. 07094
In Canada: Canadian Manda Group, P.O. Box 920, Station U, Toronto, Ontario M8Z 5P9
Queries regarding rights and permissions should be addressed to Carol Publishing Group, 600 Madison Avenue, New York, N.Y. 10022

Carol Publishing Group books are available at special discounts for bulk purchases, for sales promotions, fund raising, or educational purposes. Special editions can be created to specifications. For details, contact Special Sales Department, Carol Publishing Group, 120 Enterprise Avenue, Secaucus, N.J. 07094

Manufactured in the United States of America
10   9   8   7   6   5   4   3   2   1

Library of Congress Cataloging-in-Publication Data

Davison, James.
    Prisoners of our past : a critical look at self-defeating
attitudes within the black community / by James Davison.
        p.   cm.
    "A Birch Lane Press book."
    ISBN 1-55972-176-6 (cloth)
    1. Afro-Americans—Psychology.   2. Afro-Americans—Attitudes.
I. Title.
E185.625.D38   1993
155.8′496073—dc20   92-38064
                                                          CIP

To
Dr. George A. Johnson
and
Rev. Dr. Henry H. Nichols

Thanks, guys.

Contents

Preface

Why do black people continue to experience difficulties in getting ahead? Why do programs designed to help seem to fail miserably? What keeps black people poor, generation after generation? How are some black individuals able to attain success, while others continue to experience failure? Is it society's problem or their problem? Will things ever change?

America is presented with a confusing picture of black communities and race relations. At a time when black people are becoming increasingly visible on the national scene, there remain gross inequities between races.

All of us have heard—almost incessantly—of the societal constraints that purportedly work against black people. Prejudice, racism, discrimination, and the legacy of slavery are proffered as obstacles to success for many blacks. Grieviously, these obstacles have become cultural legacies in black communities and are reinforced in the rearing of black children. Blacks are taught that they are the victims of economic and social injustices and that educated and prosperous blacks have "sold out" (that they are Uncle Toms). Unfortunately, many blacks accept these excuses and incorporate them into their identities.

By the time many black children reach adolescence, they are well supplied with rationalizations for their lack of effort and lack of success. Outmoded family and commu-

nity influences often contribute to perpetuate poverty and
failure for black individuals. Community attitudes toward
success tend to isolate the very people the black community might expect to turn to for answers. For example, I am
a young, black, male psychologist, but this status is so
antithetical to community expectations of black males that,
in many circles, I am treated as an outsider, an Uncle Tom.

Such attitudes contribute to self-defeat for black individuals, and, given the mettle and resolution in the history of
black Americans, such attitudes are unacceptable. Black
people have been successful under much worse conditions than those that exist in this country today. Present
circumstances pale in comparison to what black people
encountered fifty, one hundred, or three hundred years
ago. Moreover, the excuses and rationalizations negate the
struggles of present and future black individuals.

These and other significant and recurrent themes in
black communities prompted me to write this book. *Prisoners of Our Past* addresses issues of self-defeat in black
communities. Information drawn from ghetto life, the process of achievement, social and clinical psychology, and
clinical practice are meant to lend flavor and substance to
the text. Ameliorative strategies toward success and freedom are offered to help ghetto inhabitants, as well as their
supporters, address the behaviors and attitudes that lead
to self-defeat and chronic poverty.

If excuses, rationalizations, and other self-defeating behaviors continue unabated, then the future of significant
segments of the black community will, without a doubt,
grow bleaker.

The author is grateful to typists Jane Finley, Margaret Hooker, and Vickie Siebert, and to Denise O'Sullivan for her expert editing. As well, I would like to thank Marion Smith for running critical interference, and for the blue cabin.

Prisoners of Our Past

1 _____

A Ghetto Fable

> Yesterday I dared to struggle, Today I dared to win.
>
> —Bernadette Devlin

I attended a traditional elementary school in a poor black neighborhood. One of my early memories is of fidgeting as my mother rubbed lard on my arms, legs, and face. She didn't want me to go to school all ashy, and lard was much less expensive than lotion. So instead I would go to school shiny and greasy. Some days she would apply lard that had already been used in cooking. I was terrified that a classmate would recognize the aroma and remark that my family had had fried chicken for dinner the night before. We were poor. We used mayonnaise jars for drinking glasses, and on many days I walked to school with holes in the soles of my shoes. And we were beleaguered. In junior high school, I often took the long way home to avoid neighborhood gangs.

Given these elements in the drama, the conventional wisdom would have it that I was destined for menial labor or prison, ball park or cabaret, or the morgue. That none of the possibilities eventuated is not owed to luck, or to the benefactions of some unknown and unseen patron, but to something else entirely. For lack of a better word, I will call it determination.

At a relatively early age I decided not to be limited by what and who was around me. It was important that I develop beyond my peers and role models. So I stayed home and studied instead of going to parties or hanging out with the fellas. I didn't join gangs or use drugs or rob people. I didn't steal cars or fancy myself a budding professional athlete or entertainer. My friends, somehow blind to the warnings that flashed before them, seemed hellbent on unfruitful and impotent lives. Most of my life was spent "getting my foot in the door," that is, trying to get the opportunity to demonstrate my worthiness for new goals and horizons. My watchword was "Just let me get my foot in the door. Just let me get in. Once I get in, I'll do well."

I believed that perseverance would help me to overcome. No matter what situations or obstacles presented themselves, I knew that I would persevere. This has always been a central and crucial aspect of my personality. Although I grew up with the same difficulties as most of my peers, I differed in one significant respect: I was determined to succeed. I believed the American credo: If a person works hard enough, he can accomplish anything.

I also decided not to be constrained by the expectations of the larger society or by my own culture and community. Both seemed to have obstacles set to thwart me. Both seemed prepared to burst the dreams and aspirations of a little black boy. But I wasn't buying it. If success would not come to me readily, then I would just persist until I won. Black or white, those who opposed me were in for a long battle. And I *would* win.

My beliefs were confirmed. The dreams and aspirations of a poor ghetto child were fulfilled. Today I am a licensed psychologist with a private clinical practice. I have worked as a consulting psychologist for numerous organizations and served on faculty at several universities. My work has been published in a number of scholarly journals, and I look forward to larger successes.

I, like the majority of my ghetto peers, could have suc-
cumbed to self-defeating behavior. I could have complained about the obstacles set against me, as my childhood friends are still inclined to do, but these obstacles
seemed laughable. Their existence was predictable and,
therefore, in my estimation, controllable. I would not be
trapped by prejudice, racism, discrimination, and the legacy of slavery. For me, they became inconsequential.

I suppose that I could lament the lack of positive role
models, the dirt and filth of the streets, being reared in a
female-headed household, and growing up on public assistance. But who cares? The important thing is to overcome.

As an individual who has "overcome," two questions that
I hear recurrently are "What made you different?" and
"How were you able to do well?" These questions are asked
by all people concerned with the disparate numbers of
blacks in varied professional fields. Frustrated by the legions of blacks who have not gained access to roads of
success, questioners typically want black professionals to
offer an explanation.

For my own part, I find people are keen to discuss the
road that I took *to become*. They want to hear my story.
And they want to know why other blacks can't seem to
make it. Sadly, in these situations, I am treated very much
as an anomaly, a sport, a rare conjunction of favorable
sociological, educational, and historical conditions.

Such conversations are very disturbing to me. First, I am
not an anomaly. The people with whom I matured were as
bright and as sharp as I. They just failed to demonstrate the
perseverance or the strength to break free of *systemic*,
personal, and cultural constraints. Many of my peers gave
up and so languished in the communities. Second, black
professionals in different fields are increasing in number,
although at what seems an excruciatingly slow pace. We
are indeed becoming less anomalous.

Like me, these black professionals are asked to tell their
stories. Both listener and teller seem to like stories that are
uncommon. The listeners like to hear stories in which the

hero overcomes adversity, as in Abe Lincoln's yarn of walking five miles in the snow for books. In the ghetto version of
the story the obstacles are insufficient food, inadequate
clothing, gangs, drugs, and a lack of positive role models.

Persons who do not achieve also cherish their stories.
Their stories of difficulties become a part of their identities,
so much so that the tellers have trouble moving away from
them. They become trapped by their saga. Sometimes it is
so difficult to move away from our stories that we may
choose not to strive for something better. Achievement may
be too foreign to our storied identities as impoverished
persons. The consideration of achievement may actually
represent the prospect of identity confusion.

These stories become a type of personal folklore, gaining
in authenticity the more often they are recounted. A typical
story:

> I'm black, and I'm poor. Most of the people I know are
> black and poor, so I suppose I'm not destined to have
> much. Our family didn't always know where our next
> meal was coming from. Dad was never around much.
> Momma was the strength of the family. Sometimes I'd
> go to school hungry and with holes in my clothes.

Unfortunately, our personal and community folklore
may, at times, cause us to hang on tenaciously to simpler,
predictable, and sanctioned existences, rather than gam-
bling on challenging and unpredictable futures. Holding
on to those simpler times or identifying with folklore keeps
us from grasping our future. It's out there. Just grab it!

2

Nurturing Defeatism

Not in the clamor of the crowded street,
Not in the shouts and plaudits of the throng,
But in ourselves, are triumph and defeat.
　　—Henry Wadsworth Longfellow, "The Poets"

Scene: TWO BLACK WOMEN ON A STREET CORNER

GAIL: Did you hear that Charlene got a good job working for
　　the city?
ROBERTA: Yeah, I heard. I can't stand her. She thinks since
　　she went to school, got some training, and some piece of
　　job, that she's something big. She acts like she's white.
　　And she tries to talk so proper. I hate her.
GAIL: Damn, you're hard on the girl.
ROBERTA: Yeah, well, she deserves it. Being Miss Ann.

As achievers move concertedly toward higher goals, they
will encounter some people who are supportive and help-
ful. These supporters give help to those in the *process of
becoming.* The help that they give, however, is not always
financial. Other forms of support, such as encouragement,
are usually more valuable than money. For many who
support achievers, that is all that they can afford to give.
And in most cases the effects of encouragement are more

enduring than the immediate but transitory effects of money.

Throughout my own process of becoming, for example, I never wanted people to shower me with money, but I always appreciated a drizzle of verbal and emotional encouragement. For me, that initial encouragement was offered by my third-grade teacher. She imbued in me a motivation toward excellence, and she taught me to enact and pursue my dreams. More important, she validated my efforts.

Many people can tell similar stories of some individual who, perhaps unknowingly, greatly influenced them. Such supporters and helpers may not themselves have had the opportunity to advance during their youth. Perhaps their own processes of becoming were curtailed by marriage, the arrival of children, lack of positive reinforcement, inadequate role modeling, finances, and so on, but through the activities of those they benefact they are able to live vicariously.

Parents, of course, traditionally serve in the role of cheerleader. For instance, a child may decide to become something more than was expected of her—mechanic, scholar, restaurateur, teacher. Her parents may make sacrifices, provide positive reinforcement, and in many other ways foster an environment in which that child's dream becomes possible. For example, her father may drive her to the library three times each week to get books. Her mother may spend more time than usual helping with homework. As a result of their efforts, her parents may bask in the light of their child's future achievements. They can take pride in the fruit of their planning and nurturance.

Through this process the child, and likely her own children, may do a little better than her parents. Ideally each successive generation should be better off than the last. Whether academic or entrepreneurial, this process of sequential achievement represents the quintessence of upward mobility for ethnic minorities in the United States.

Historically, members of ethnic minority groups and women have experienced significant and chronic difficulties in their efforts toward upward mobility. Under some conditions, however, highly motivated individuals from these groups have been able to burst the bonds that constrain them. Women, for example, enjoy increased success in medical schools; blacks today experience increased success in fields other than athletics and entertainment.

But such success is not without a price. Often, in their quest to achieve, these highly motivated persons must endure considerable abuse from the communities to which they aspire. Prejudice, racism, sexism, and discrimination are some of the abuses that achievers must face. As well, the attitude of the achiever's native community can be influential. A negative response to initial achievements can be a serious impediment to future success.

Unfortunately, as there are community members who are supportive of achievers, there are also those who choose to detract.

Scene: TWO BLACK MEN ON A STREET CORNER

GREG: Yo, homes, what's up?

JEROME: Yo, I've been trying to catch up with you forever. Man, I got accepted to the university. I'm going to get my college degree, and hopefully a good job.

GREG: Man, what's up with that? You know those white people don't want you there. And if they did, they just using your black ass as a token.

JEROME: You think so?

GREG: Yo, all they got down there is white people. You may have gotten in, but ain't no way your ass is gonna graduate. [*Pause*] Hey, I wouldn't shit you. This one dude went there—they abused the brother. Ended up a crackhead.

JEROME: No shit!?

GREG: Yo. You gotta watch your back, because they ain't gonna help you.

One might think that as some members of a group try to improve their lot, other members would encourage them and show support. Irrespective of the sphere of legitimate endeavor, one might reasonably expect a spirit of well-being and positive reinforcement or, as a minimum, indifference. However, in many situations those who have not put forth the effort to achieve act like crabs in a basket. That is, as one crab tries to claw its way out, another pulls it back. As a result, no crab or only the truly exceptional, can escape.

In black communities, individuals who dash the hopes of others are all too common. Nonachievers must, at some level, decry the successes of achievers. People who climb out of the basket bring the inability or unwillingness of others to do likewise, into the light. Achievers successes may likely represent a significant threat to the self-esteem and sense of efficacy of nonachievers. Some nonachievers address this threat by minimizing the successes of climbers. They cite chance, luck, or preferential treatment as central factors in the success of their peers. Others vilify achievers by denouncing their connection to the community, thereby, nonachievers are able to dismiss any comparative judgments between themselves and achievers. Rather than rejoicing in a person's standing or achievement, they impugn: "He's an Uncle Tom (Aunt Sally)." "You're trying to out-white the white folks." "She's trying to be white." "Miss Ann." "Oreo." Antagonistically they deny or dismiss the achievements of group members and declare the achievers misguided or compromised.

From a social psychological perspective, it is not difficult to understand the motivation of those who seek to hold back the climbers. They, like most people want to see themselves in a positive light. They wish to view themselves as good, success-oriented, effectual persons, individuals who want to better themselves. At the same time, they want others to see them as good, success-oriented individuals. By acknowledging the successes of one's peers, nonachievers would concomitantly admit their own defeats.

Alternative to the pulling back of climbers, nonachievers may also avoid threats to self-esteem and efficacy by redefining success, equating it with the unqualified earning of money. But success entails more than the mere accumulation of cash. This lesson seems absent in the rearing of many black children. Pimps, drug dealers, and other hustlers are able to accumulate enormous amounts of cash. They can buy virtually any of the accouterments of the upper socioeconomic classes, but will never be afforded the concomitant social status. One must be able to afford a disassociation from ghetto mentality and its detrimental effects.

Scene: TWO TEENAGE BOYS SITTING ON A STOOP IN THE COOL, COOL, COOL OF A SUMMER'S EVENING

CHRIS: Yo, homey. You going to that party on Friday?

LARRY: Word! I'm not missing that. It's going to be hipe. Lots of beer and lots of honeys.

CHRIS: I know. I'm trying to talk my moms into getting me something to wear.

LARRY: Yo! Your moms still taking you shopping? Later for that. I take myself shopping, and I'm hipe. [*Larry turns slowly, arms outstretched, in a modeling pivot.*] Whenever I want to go shopping, I go shopping. Yo, I keep some money. [*Larry fishes out about three hundred dollars in twenties, while stuffing remainder of the cash back in his pants pocket.*] And my moms don't say shit about it.

CHRIS [wide-eyed]: Yo, where'd you get all that money?

LARRY: Yo, a man's gotta do what a man's gotta do.

CHRIS: What do you mean? Why can't you tell me?

LARRY: Hey, it ain't exactly legal, and I know how your family is. Churchgoing and all that.

CHRIS: Well, you're right. [*Pause*] Damn, that's a lot of money. Tell me how you got it anyway, man.

One pays a price in order to be disassociated from ghetto

mentality while living in the ghetto. The price is most often an ostracism of sorts—requiring the sacrifice of peer relationships, social approval, affiliation, and ease of identity formation. In effect, the individual must develop an identity somewhat separate from ghetto influences. This hefty price is worth paying when one considers the alternatives: chronic social and economic difficulties and retarded self-development. It is unconscionable to blame an individual for the circumstances to which he or she is born. But if that individual does not assume his or her responsibility as a social participant in the larger society, he or she only serves to perpetuate debilitating circumstances within the community. Too often ghetto inhabitants restrict their interactions to the ghetto. They resign themselves to the limitations of their surroundings and ghetto expectations of success. Such resignation affects not only them, but also their children and their children and, ultimately, the entire community.

In ghetto cultures, the goal of intergenerational advancement—the essence of the American dream—has been seriously derailed by the immediacy of consumerism. Many people aspire simply to ride in the Benz (which has supplanted the Caddy), wear gold, and dress GQ. Black people who are poor can ill afford to be caught in a struggle for the acquisition of objects. Their ability to purchase objects will inevitably become increasingly compromised as their education, training, and entrepreneurship continue to decline in relation to the demands of consumerism. Middle-class America values (and acquires) education, training, and entrepreneurship, as well as consumer items. Many black people, however, seem only to value the latter. Perhaps their skewed values are created through a perceived lack of access to education, training, and business. But the inaccessibility is really a misperception. After acquiring education, training, and business, consumer items will follow, and with much less sacrifice than is now experienced.

Too often, black children grow up with many contradictory influences competing for their souls. Alongside the admonitions of those adults who regard education, training, and planning as important are the allurements of adults who offer fathomless and immediate material satisfaction. The children are warned about the pitfalls of street life. But the seeming success of some of their peers often entices them. These youths are confused about which life to pursue. On the one hand, they face the prospect of deferred reinforcement as they train for years so that one day, maybe, they will obtain a forty-thousand-dollar-a-year-job. With this prospect they look forward to enacting the American dream—mortgages, children, cars, and other expenses that will strain their wallets. On the other hand, by aligning with more lowdown types, they can immediately obtain enormous amounts of cash to do with as they please. They can command the respect of some of their peers now rather than all of them at some future time.

Their choices are further complicated by the preponderance of role models who are profitably engaged in nefarious and illicit activity. Examples of success through drug businesses, prostitution, pimping, and other criminal activity abound, while examples of "overcoming" through legitimate and nonstereotypical activities seem to go unnoticed. How can responsible adults, often of lower economic status than "outlaw" community members, hope to compete for the souls of these children?

Scene: TWO BOYS HAVING LUNCH IN CAFETERIA OF A PREDOMINANTLY BLACK HIGH SCHOOL

LOUIS: Yo, Ronnie. You ain't been in class for a week. What's up?

RONNIE: Yo, I'm tired of school. It's stupid.

LOUIS: You was cool with it last week.

RONNIE: Yeah, but it finally hit me. Like, my pops keeps tellin' me to do good in school because that's the only way to get ahead.

LOUIS: Yo, my parents say the same thing.

RONNIE: Yeah, but my pops been workin' hard all his life, and what the niggah got to show for it? [*Pause*] Nothing. Still rentin' some stupid crib, four kids, livin' sorry-ass paycheck to sorry-ass paycheck. Workin' nights just to keep some food on the table.

LOUIS: Yo, least he's respectable, brother. Don't do no drugs or drink. Least he's trying.

RONNIE: Man, who cares? It's all about crazy dollars. All anybody concerned about in this world is the cash. [*Pause*] Try to buy some clothes, or take a girl out, or buy your moms a present with respect. You'd get your ass kicked out of the store. But step in there with some serious cash, and you hold check. Believe me, they don't care where it comes from.

LOUIS: Yeah, man, but—

RONNIE: But nothin', Louis. I'm tired of goin' to school just to get hassled by teachers and gettin' robbed in the hallways while other niggahs gettin' rich sellin' drugs and shit. I want in on some of that cash.

LOUIS: Yo. You better take care.

RONNIE: For what? It's all about the future, my brother. This stuff is for losers. [*Ronnie turns to leave*]

LOUIS: Where you goin' now?

RONNIE: Gonna go talk to T-Bone.

LOUIS [shocked]: The crack man?

RONNIE [*exasperated by his friend's naïveté*]: Hey, Louis. T-Bone is ridin' around in a Benz while we walkin'. My brother must be doing somethin' right.

One of the most important factors that seems to differentiate the choices these children make is the values at home. Children from homes where positive social values are jointly developed and discussed are probably less likely to succumb to street life than children from homes where criminality is tolerated or encouraged. The former will ascribe to values not limited by money. The latter will be subject to becoming engaged in any quick money-making opportunities.

For me, I couldn't wait until I had the opportunity to develop, grow, and move beyond the nearsightedness of much of my community. Peers seemed to talk of little but the last swinging party, the next opportunity to get high, sex, and how to score "big money." They seemed unable or unwilling to look beyond the events of the current week. A person cannot see the future if he doesn't open his eyes to values beyond cash and street life.

Street life, however, represents only one of the dangerous choices children may make. Alternate to those persons who choose the street life are those persons who choose to yield unconditionally to the complacency of the ghetto. These individuals resign themselves to lack of access, lack of opportunity, and lack of prosperity. They come to believe that the system is powerfully pitted against them. And this belief, much more than the peculiarities of the system, is their downfall. They, like their street-life counterparts, are peripheral to the normal discourse of American society. And such persons defeat themselves.

3

Breeding Grounds

> It is a consolation to the wretched to have com-
> panions in misery.
>
> —Publius Syrus Maxim 995

The street corner serves as a waiting and initiation area for young black males. Many sell drugs; others wait for gang action. From sunrise to sunset, one may witness the huddled interaction of these men. It may be likened to the changing of a work shift when, at daybreak, the younger men relinquish their spots to older, alcohol seekers.

Scene: TWO MEN ON A WINDY STREET CORNER

TYRELL: Shit! The hawk's out today.

CHESTER: You ain't lyin', man. When's this dive going to open up?

TYRELL: Hey, man, just yesterday he was late and I had to straighten the dude out. I said, "You running a business or not?"

CHESTER: I heard that. We spend too much money up in this shithole to be kept waiting. I hope he gets his ass here. I got to go downtown this morning. My girl got me an interview for some piece of job. Just barely above minimum. I got to be there by nine. [*Pause*] Come on, man. Open up! Shit! I just needs a little taste before the inter-

14

view. [*Pause*] Hey, my brother, can you help me out with some change so I can get downtown?

TYRELL: Nigger, you crazy. Got just enough to get me something to drink. Look, why you even going? Shit. Minimum wage? You got to make mo money'n that. White man's always trying to work niggers for nothing. I ain't taking no damned job for less'n thirty thou.

In every large city in the United States scores of black, uneducated, and alcoholic middle-aged males wait for the local tavern to open at 6:45 in the morning. While their peers enjoy their best years professionally and financially, these men spend their time and egos in taverns. Every day you see the same helplessness and self-delusion. For those foreign to the community, it is difficult to imagine the scope of the problem. It used to be that only the winos and rummies would hang out *that* early in the morning. But today, disturbingly, there has been a rise in the number of young black males (ages twenty-five to forty) who also wait for the neighborhood tavern to open—no doubt following in the footsteps of their role models.

Taverns have been, for many years, crucial centers of socialization and interaction for black males. After a long day at work, men would stop off on their way home for "a drink or two with the fellas." Today, however, the unemployed are doing most of the drinking. Frequenting the bar has become a full-time job. (In even worse condition are those who buy their daily quart or two of beer at the local convenience store and drink it alone.)

The unemployed, the underemployed, and the unemployable have become disillusioned with their futures and, in frustration, have turned to drink, at the tavern or alone, to find self-esteem or companionship. Their lack of employment is perpetuated by a lack of motivation, by poor achievement orientation, by a paucity of what they consider acceptable role models, and by never-ending delusions. These men are, in essence, standing still while the rest of the world is moving forward. They are, without a doubt, losing ground economically, socially, and emotionally. These men, who can ill afford to maintain the status quo, are doing so with a vengeance.

The tavern (or street corner or gang) serves as the arena in which basic social psychological needs (affiliation, self-esteem enhancement, love) are addressed. Unfortunately the men who congregate there have erroneously concluded that they cannot gain access to more bountiful spheres of interaction and endeavor, so they look to the tavern to address those needs.

For instance, individuals may feel alone and desire the company of friends with whom they have something in common. Under normal circumstances, most people address such affiliative needs through involvement with groups from work or school or church or lodge. But those who have eliminated these spheres from their lives address the needs through involvement with tavern patrons. For the underaged, the involvement may be with violent gangs and criminals.

The vehicle through which this need for affiliation is met—whatever the name—is irrelevant. Gangs, taverns, and criminal organizations address the same affiliative needs addressed in churches, jobs, and families. Affiliation is affiliation. It doesn't matter whether it is effected through the corporation, the college dormitory, or the bar stool. That the need is addressed—whatever the method—is paramount.

Chronic tavern, street-corner, or gang interaction, however, eventuates in a sort of generalized depression. We do not necessarily mean the kind of depression that may lead to a suicide attempt. Rather, it is a depression of resignation—a melancholia. This depression often pervades many different aspects of the person's life. He may strike out emotionally at family, friends, or strangers. He may feign uncaring attitudes, establish chronic patterns of irresponsibility, and blame others for his shortcomings; all are manifestations of his depression. His lack of efficacy in spheres other than the tavern is reinforced through rationalization, self-delusion, and a collusive spirit with other frequenters of the tavern. Within the tavern walls, he has worth and purpose and is an integral contributor to its society and social discourse. Outside the tavern, in many spheres, he is ineffectual. The universal unspoken tavern rule applies: "If you don't step on my rationalizations and delusions, I won't step on yours."

Scene: TOURING RICK'S TAVERN

YOUR GUIDE: Roland, how you doing today?

ROLAND [*a would-be basketball star*]: Oh, I'm just here chillin', watchin' the game.

YOUR GUIDE: Who's playing?

ROLAND: The Knicks and Sixers. [*Pause*] Man, look at that dude. He ain't shit. When I played ball in school I did the same shit he's doin'. Man, I could take that dude to the hoop.

YOUR GUIDE: Yeah?

ROLAND: Aw, man, I used to hoop! [*Stated emphatically, with each and every appropriate accompanying hand and body gesture*] I took everybody to the hoop. Hey, Bobby! Tell 'em, man!

BOBBY: Yeah.

ROLAND: I was bad! You hear me, bad! I practiced day and night, night and day. I always had a basketball with me. It was like a full-time gig, man. I *was* the team. They wasn't shit without me. Huh, Bobby?

BOBBY: That one white boy on the team was pretty good.

ROLAND: Man, I'll smack you. What you talkin' about? You know damned well I was *it*.

BOBBY: Yeah, okay, man.

ROLAND: If I hadn't messed up my knee, you'd be watching me on TV instead of me sittin' up here in this bar talking to these sorry mothers. [*Pause*] Damn, I wish I had finished school or got some kind of trade or something. Yeah. My moms kept telling me to have something to fall back on. Shit.

[*Enter two women*]

ROLAND [*leaning to the side*]: Hey, baby, what's your name? Damn, you're fine. Damn! Who you here with, baby? [*No response*]

Bitch! She's probably a dyke anyway. Thinks she's too good for me. Like somebody wants her ass. [*Pause*]

What were we talkin' about? Oh, yeah. I was on the way up. Was goin' to buy my moms a new house. You know you gotta take care of Moms. Then get me a bad car, some clothes, and two or three hoes. Shit just fell apart, man. [*Pregnant pause*]

Aw, man, he just missed a bullshit layup. Told you the dude wasn't shit.

[*Enter Maurice, a would-be singer*]

Missed opportunities abound as the beat of rationalization syncopates loudly. People are so busy protecting their sense of efficacy and self-esteem that the defenses that shield them keep them from grabbing at opportunities. For example, if one believes that "the white man is always trying to work niggers for nothing," then the groundwork for self-defeat is laid down. One must be willing to start somewhere in order to move. Unfortunately, too many blacks refuse to get on the ladder. They relish interaction with those of their ilk; they wait for the proverbial forty acres and a mule. And, in waiting, they teach and show their children the obscenities of defeatism.

Scene: YOUNG BOY RETURNING HOME AFTER MORNING AT A FRIEND'S HOUSE

JUNIOR: Hi, Mom.

MOM: Hi, Junior. Did you have fun over at Greg's house?

JUNIOR [*hesitantly*]: It was okay, Mom.

MOM: What's wrong, Junior? Did something happen over there? Tell me; what's wrong?

JUNIOR: Mom! Nothing happened. You're always worrying too much.

MOM: Are you sure? It's okay. You can tell me.

JUNIOR: I don't want Greg to get in any trouble or anything.

MOM: It's okay, Junior. Tell me.

JUNIOR: Well, we were upstairs playing with his new train set, and his mom busted in and started talking crazy and yelling at him for nothing.

MOM: What was she yelling about?

JUNIOR: I don't know. She was just yelling and not making sense. And she smelled funny.

MOM: Smelled funny? Like what?

JUNIOR: I don't know, Mom. Just funny. Later when we went downstairs, she was in the living room smoking this tiny little cigarette and passing it around to about four or five other people who were there. The smoke smelled funny, and it kinda made my throat itch.

MOM: What did Greg say?

JUNIOR: He didn't really say nothing. He just got kinda quiet. And I didn't really ask him anything because I didn't want to be rude.

MOM: Good. That's good.

JUNIOR: And then down the street we saw his older brother, Eddie. I think I smelled that same smell on him, too. I asked Greg could he smell it and what it was. But he kept his head down and started kicking rocks. He asked could he come over here to play, but I told him I needed permission first.

MOM: Junior, I don't think I want you going over there anymore. I mean, Greg is nice, and you and he can still be friends, but be friend outside his house. You boys can come over here and play if you want to or if it's raining or something.

JUNIOR: I'll call him right now. He's a nice person. He just needs someplace where he can play.

MOM [*thinking*]: And grow.

Whether among one's relatives, on a street corner, or at home, waiting exacts an enormous price from black adults and children. This is particularly the case when we mitigate the wait through drug and alcohol use. Although drug and alcohol addictions have grievous effects on users, the long-term effects upon children are worse. Children must pass users on the streets every day, must sometimes live in their homes—victims to users' erratic behavior. They must avoid the shards of green glass that were once bottles of cheap wine. They see the empty beer bottles on their way to school, church, and library. Vials, glassine bags, and the other paraphernalia of narcotics litter their playgrounds.

As our children look to adults for models, leadership, and guidance, they are often met and crushed by indifference, rage, and weakness. Whether children choose to embrace or avoid the culture of self-defeat, these adult models, in their intoxicated wait, have an untoward effect upon their children's development and psyches.

4

Crab, Lobster, and Other Seafood: Climbing Out of the Basket

> Envy is a pain of mind that successful men cause their neighbors.
> —Onasander the General

Personally, it was important for me to leave "the community" in order *to become*. I was tired of the dirt, the crime, and the threats. Two major dangers for me and other black males were gang warfare and the police. One could be pressed into service by the gang, thereby avoiding harassment or even death. Actually, a conscription system of sorts worked to protect the gang's interests. I avoided the police by staying out of trouble, not hanging out in the streets, and not presenting a challenge to them. Many of the police officers who worked in my neighborhood were suspicious and disdainful of black males. Their menacing patrols, wanton harassment, and capricious arrests of my friends served as continual reminders of the lack of respect and recourse accorded black males in the United States society.

There's no denying I felt I lived among monsters. Some

21

wore gang colors, some dwelt in red-and-white patrol cars. They loomed everywhere. These monsters seemed stationed to retard and impede my progress out of the ghetto. To survive into adulthood, I had to learn how to most effectively avoid these beasts.

However, before I could begin to free myself, there remained two considerations. First, a general inertia that seemed to clutch at my ankles but operated in my mind, an inertia that reduced my motivation to act. Some of this inertia can be attributed to a lack of appropriate role models or peer relations. But much more may be explained by a general and pervasive acceptance of conditions, a disdain for those who choose to move out, and a reinforcing collusive spirit held by many members of the community. These debilitating and insidious dangers continue as ever-present and growing powers in black communities.

The second consideration was my daring to strike out on my own. I had to proclaim to self and others my independence from the limitations of my surroundings. As a result, I rejected those black community values that limited me. I had to also learn to ignore the inevitable racial impasses awaiting me down the road.

As I matured, I became less concerned with the expectations, norms, and values of those around me and more concerned about internal standards. These internal standards were functional, enduring, and consistent with success. All too often, the community (external) standards reinforced failure. It is difficult to appreciate the level of effort exerted *to become* by those reared in debilitating circumstances. They must negotiate through problems from both pluralistic and nonpluralistic spheres as they strive upward. That is, not only must they armor themselves to battle with traditions that have effectively excluded black people from coveted spheres, but at the same time they must deflect the attacks of black persons who would keep them mired in less fertile fields.

Popular folklore has it that poor, oppressed, repressed,

downtrodden, uneducated, and underemployed persons have a more difficult row to hoe than others. I beg to take serious exception to that notion. I truly believe that the road toward success is much more difficult, emotionally and psychologically, for striving individuals than for those persons who choose not to strive, but only to survive. Achievers have chosen to wage the battle and struggle toward emotional, economic, and spiritual independence. They do so while trying to tolerate and survive their present conditions, all in the face of significant resistance from institutions where high levels of prejudice and discrimination have lain unchallenged and entrenched for decades.

To sally forth into such a fray requires considerable resolve and emotional wherewithal, particularly when the achiever must battle without the support (or worse, with the reproof) of his community of origin. Unquestionably it is less difficult not to try than to try. Not to try only requires that one rationalize the lack of effort or motivation, while maintaining the status quo. This strategy of active entrenchment has enjoyed its heyday in segments of the black community. But it's time for a change.

For many black persons, the *process of becoming* is fraught with ambivalence. In my clinical practice, I regularly meet persons who are "making it" economically and professionally but who experience difficulties socially.

In the typical example, the man works downtown and is successful in his field. Still, he feels an inexplicable pull toward the expectations of the "homies" with whom he grew up. He finds himself hanging out with shady characters or dabbling in a little nefarious activity or just plain screwing up. He engages in activities that have the potential of compromising his present life-style. Often this individual is troubled with identity problems. He does not feel solidly connected to either his homies or his professional associates.

According to the client, his homies don't understand his professional life because they have never approached or entertained the idea of a professional career. And his professional colleagues do not have a clue about his background and experiences. Although his homies don't know him as he is now, he, at least, knows them. And off he goes to rejoin them, to fit in. However, this attempt to fit in with the brothers proves to be restrictive, often depressing. Their existence is a tragic one because they haven't changed, at all. His own existence is so unlike theirs that he eventually comes to feel disconnected from them. Not fitting in anywhere is difficult to come to terms with.

This may partially account for the "you can't go home again" philosophy espoused by some black people. Too many years and events have passed. Home, as you knew it, no longer exists, and you have changed.

When black professionals decide to "go home" (that is, reach out to the masses), they are seldom met with an overflow of embracing acceptance. Many respond instead with apprehension, jealousy, resentment, or indifference. More often than not, black scholars and professionals are ostracized by black communities. This ostracism often contributes to identity concerns for those black persons who are affected by racial or community edicts. That is, black professionals and others are, many times, at odds with what their racial peers deem exemplary "black behavior." One need only think of the long-standing rift between the black middle-class and the "masses." For those persons at odds, identity issues command a recurrent significance.

As an adolescent, I sometimes endeavored to remain current with all the vernacular, behavior, and fashion that identified me as a member in good standing in the community. With regard to vernacular and behavior, this presented few problems. I had only to pick up the latest phrase or physical affectation, and I was set. I spoke all the jargon. I knew all the "gets" (up, down, over, funky, and loose) and all the "what's" (up, happening, shaking, it look like, going down, it be like). I purchased and sold "wolf tickets," sported (wore) "rags" and "vines," and was often in need of "scratch." Furthermore, I could "stroll with a dip" and ask a girl if I could "stand a chance." However, I was not very adept at "holding my hands," so I rarely "called anyone out." I stopped short of having a "process," due to interminably short hair, but did work on my "waves."

However, my flair for fashion fell short. Keeping abreast of the latest trends in the world of black haute couture was quite expensive, and my family was poor. For example, the boys began to wear slacks that we called "silk and wools." Having a pair of silk and wools elevated you instantly to the status of *cool*. In point of fact, no self-respecting homeboy would be caught at a house party without his silk and wools, Italian knit (a type of shirt-sweater combination), and either Italian loafers, Presidents, or ass-kickers. Attention to fashion even extended to athletic arenas, where Chuck Taylors (high tops, of course) were the rage. All in an effort to fit in and be one of the boys.

I, however, rarely found my attire or appurtenances fashionable. For example, I always wore cuffed blue jeans, not for the trend but, at that time, the low cost. (Serendipitously, I found my clothes became fashionable every few years as the fad pendulum swung back in my direction.) Although not fashionable, I had style.

No doubt every culture has its own particular fashion trends, particularly within the adolescent crowd. It just always struck me as strange that people who could least afford it would afford it. I suppose social scientists and theoreticians would assert that individuals and groups who traditionally have enjoyed little access to the benefits of the general culture nonetheless identify with the culture.

Poor people often look to the larger culture for direction and values. As with all groups, they become motivated to acquire the larger culture's most valued and attractive appurtenances. Not to be outdone by their more financially solvent counterparts, many poor black people seek and covet the objects advertised as trappings of upper-middle-class American culture. Like everyone else, they purchase VCRs and new cars and aspire to high fashion.

The influence of culture extends beyond general culture. Subgroups, like black communities, also exert considerable influence upon their members. Culture contributes greatly to what we consider to be our "personal" goals and identities. Peer relations are especially important to identity during adolescence, but adulthood demands more discernment. The community standards that one views as suitable should be incorporated into one's life-style, and unsuitable standards should be disregarded. Such choices may seem quite risky to those black persons who are already experiencing marginality. However, failing to make reasoned choices for one's life-style can perpetuate cultural and racial dissociation.

I decided to value myself and not to subscribe to anyone else's idea of who I should be. For me, both "black" culture and the general culture had aspects to avoid. I decided to fashion my own culture. Taking from any and all cultures what was important for me, I became increasingly comfortable with my developing self. More comfortable than I had been while buying into what I had then perceived as either *black* culture or *white* culture. One's sense of self should not emanate solely from community-orientation, or black orientation, or church orientation, or whatever orientation. Each is inconsequential. None is more important than any other. One must determine the relative value of each orientation for himself and incorporate his choices.

Scene: AFTER A PARENTS' MEETING AT A BLACK NEIGHBORHOOD SCHOOL

MS. JOHNSON: Dr. Davison, I thoroughly enjoyed your presentation to our parents' group.

DR. DAVISON: Well, I hope I was of some assistance in helping your group with its goals.

MS. JOHNSON: Oh, yes. And as you were speaking I thought that you would make a good role model for the children at this school. [*Pause*] But I'm afraid you might be a little too different from them.

DR. DAVISON: Different? I'm not sure I know what you mean.

MS. JOHNSON: Lord knows, we need positive black male role models in this community. Lord knows. And you would make a good one, except . . .

DR. DAVISON: Except what? I'm still uncertain what you mean. Please be more specific.

MS. JOHNSON: Well, you're positive and you speak well, but you are a little too much like *them*.

DR. DAVISON [*dumbfounded*]: *Them*? Who are *they*?

MS. JOHNSON: You know, white folks.

DR. DAVISON: What in the world do you mean?

MS. JOHNSON: You know. For instance, you dress like them.

DR. DAVISON: What? What are you talking about?

MS. JOHNSON: You know, like your tie. It's pretty white.

DR. DAVISON [*shocked, with the monster of sarcasm ready to rear its ugly head*]: When I went into the store I saw this tie. I *liked* this tie, so I *bought* this tie. And now I *wear* this tie. I didn't buy it to make some geopolitical statement. When I visited the clothing store, I didn't notice a section for *black* men's ties and another for *white* men's ties. I mean, should Jesse's picture be on it? You really need to lighten up.

MS. JOHNSON: You don't have to get smart! I was just saying that our kids need role models who will teach them to be *black* men and *black* women.

DR. DAVISON: And just what does that entail?

MS. JOHNSON: Well, to be strong in themselves, to know their African roots, to be good people in the community, to understand the battle with the white man, to raise children in positive ways. That sort of thing.

DR. DAVISON [*the monster of sarcasm still lurking*]: And what the hell does that have to do with my tie?

MS. JOHNSON [*walking away in a huff*]: I guess you just don't really understand the black experience.

Anything that a black person decides to do that is not destructive of other individuals or black communities should be sufficient to constitute positive role modeling. Contrary to the ravings of many, thinking for oneself is not negative or destructive to black communities. Unfortunately the range of what many persons envision as positive black role modeling is extremely confined. They suggest that black role models should speak, dress, and behave in ways that are, in fact, very limiting. They proffer that, above all else, these role models must *think* with a black community orientation. Most of us, however, have been and remain unsure of just what that orientation should be. We have been Christians, Muslims, urban warriors, Democrats, bucks, responsible Negroes, good niggers, militants, and revolutionaries. We have been angry, ingratiating, forthright, compliant, and dependent. We have been cohesive, destructive, active, stagnant, and floundering. Maybe it's time to just try becoming the best human beings that we can.

This *process of becoming* for individuals includes development and growth in academic, entrepreneurial, social, and personal spheres. It may be likened to the relationship between a child and her parents. There are a number of developmental paths the child can travel. She can internalize all parental teachings of values, goals, and beliefs. If compliant, she will become what her parents desire, an adult who reflects and engenders the values, goals, and beliefs of her parents, while developing few of her own. She may well be weak of character, indecisive, and easy prey for the machinations of any strong-willed parent figure. She may be destined to spend much of her adult life orchestrating situations through which others will parent her.

Alternatively she can choose independence. However, in order to become a complete, integrated, self-sufficient, and fully functioning adult, some rejection or incomplete internalization of parental teachings must occur. She must discover that she is an extension of her parents (or her community), and not a replica of them. If she completely and unquestioningly absorbs parental teachings (or, analogously, the teachings of the community), she will not progress to healthy adult independence, will not become self-sufficient.

As with our caretakers, we should look toward our communities with regard to their parenting functions. Individuals must strive to become extensions of their communities, not slaves to them. This issue is extremely important, because the concept of community is paramount for upwardly mobile black people.

The influence of community is, at the same time, similar and dissimilar to that found in other groups. Similarities revolve around familial desires for achievement and success. Dissimilarities revolve around how the experiences and histories of racism, classism, discrimination, slavery, and self-oppression through community entrenchment have functioned to compromise the enactment of those desires.

Most of us want good things for ourselves. We want to be successful, happy, and fully functioning adults in our professions and home lives. Unfortunately, for many black persons, the notion of *the unfair system* has become a truism. Many black people compromise their futures by not attempting to reap the system's benefits. This is a particularly peculiar stance when one considers that at the present time, social, financial, economic, and career opportunities for black people have never been better. Black individuals can pursue an enormous range of endeavors. However, many find themselves confused about what direction they should take.

On the one hand, black people are able to see the enormous opportunities available to them. The battles waged in the past are being won in many fields. But, on the other hand, the notion of increasing opportunities runs counter to the history and folklore of restricted access and overwhelming discrimination. This history and folklore have

been nurtured and reified to the detriment of black communities. Though there are ever-increasing opportunities
for black people in the business community, the inherent
complexity of sorting through a labyrinth of historical restraints checks the advancement of many.

Unfortunately many of us are guilty of perpetuating poverty within our community. We teach and reinforce each
other to be poor. In many circles, a persons's "blackness" is
questioned whenever his financial status is above that of
the masses of black folk. This is particularly the case when
one's financial gain results from legitimate, nonathletic,
nonentertainment, or nonhustled activity. Subsequently,
many economically secure black people feel pressed to
"prove" their blackness by contributing time, money, and
other resources to "the cause." Times are indeed confusing
when upward mobility for black individuals is hampered
by identity concerns foisted by the larger black community.

Certainly there is nothing wrong with being poor. However, contrary to popular belief, neither is there anything
wrong with being financially "better off." To think otherwise would bring into question the "blackness" of those
black persons who are coping well in the system. Such
persons represent a challenge to an oversimplified analysis
of the economic and cultural status of black persons today.

During my childhood poverty was the glue that bonded
otherwise disparate black persons together as community.
Those few who were better off financially were treated as
anomalies and peripheral to the community. When I was a
child my future prospects seemed terrifying. Sometimes I
would cry because I didn't want to be in one of the jobs
that seemed to exhaust career opportunities for black men.
A very restricted range of careers for black males was reinforced through societal expectations and, as strongly, by
my role models. This is not to diminish the struggles that
these role models experienced. They were, in all probability, similarly socialized as children. Rather, it is to sug-

gest that there must be other accepted, reinforced, and valued avenues to success.

In order for black communities to advance, the successes of professional, scholarly, and licensed persons in various fields *must* be as highly valued as the ability to slam-dunk, outsprint the opposition, or turn out a platinum album. Unfortunately, many of our children receive more encouragement in singing, dancing, and adeptness with a ball than in striving, achieving, and succeeding. Worse, some children receive no direction at all from their parents and are subject to whatever influence is strongest.

Those young persons who are able to meander or navigate through the labyrinth of historical restraints and ever-increasing present opportunity often find themselves confronting different problems. While pursuing professional careers, many black people feel suddenly not accepted wholly into either their achieved world or their ascribed world.[1] Their marginal existence can be a source of considerable distress. Are they "black," as the mirror tells them? Are they "white," as many persons in the black community intimate? Or are they developing into something different from either?

The healthiest, psychologically, opt for whatever identity that evolves. If they identify with historical restraints and compromise their opportunities, then they may feel limited and inactive in terms of their education and experiences although, sadly, in step with much of the black community. Alternatively, if they identify with their present opportunities and pursue them actively, then they may feel disconnected and sometimes in opposition to the black community at large.

Many black professionals wonder whether the struggle is worth the trouble. Few persons want to feel like outsiders.

1. Ascribed and achieved status are sociological terms that refer to the station to which one is born, and stations to which one ascends during one's lifetime, respectively.

Fewer still want to feel like or be characterized as Uncle Toms or Aunt Sallys, or uncaring. So, to remain, in their minds, members of the community in good standing, many succumb to the manipulations of community groups or leaders. They give time and money to black community efforts that often are without direction. Some feel duped by organizations. When these professionals choose not to be duped or are not readily forthcoming, disappointment and ostracism follow.

It should be obvious that black professionals provide role models and blaze trails for future travelers. In addition, their presence in their respective professions serves to acclimate institutions to the worth, values, and skills inherent in all people—including black people. Any other service that these professionals provide to black communities is gravy, worthwhile, but not essential.

Unfortunately, some community members and leaders believe that black professionals *owe* the community a debt of service or access to resources. With an air of entitlement, they commonly assert that professionals should be willing to "give back" (typically without remuneration) to the community. It appears that not only do community leaders want the services of black professionals who are knowledgeable, competent, and sensitive to community issues, but they also want them at cut rates.

I am certain that there exist those black professionals who give of themselves, unremittingly, to "the kids," "the brothers," "the sisters," "the community." I am sure that there exist as well those professionals who choose not to contribute until that contribution is received with open arms. And there must also be those professionals who just assert, "To hell with the community." For the most part my experiences have been mixed; ranging from suspicion ("What does he really want?") to skepticism and black racism ("How do we know if you're any good?") to open acceptance ("Please do whatever you can. Anything would be appreciated").

We've all heard the complaint that when black individuals "make it," they don't give back to the community. I have been asked countless times to offer my professional services to the community. The argument goes: "Don't forget where you come from. You should be willing to offer your services without fee to the brothers and sisters. Give something back to the community." I would argue that the "brothers and sisters" should be willing, if not overjoyed, to pay for the professional services of someone who comes from their ranks, with whom they may identify. My usual response is, "Would you ask a white professional to perform those services for free?" Ignore me, ostracize me, but don't pimp me.

In my opinion, black professionals don't *owe* anything. The only person who owes you anything is yourself. A number of social service programs may have fostered the posture of entitlement and dependency, but it is a posture of self-oppression. People seem content to wait for someone or some agency to give them what they are supposedly *due*. Many proffer the argument that: "Since our ancestors were enslaved, stripped of their culture, suffered familial disruptions, and historically were treated as subhuman, our economic development as a group has been delayed. So it is only fair that the group that still reaps the benefits of institutionalized racism—white people—feel guilty for the transgressions of their ancestors. Thereby, black people are owed a moral and economic debt. So, please pay up. Furthermore, those black persons who do become successful need to come back and help pull the rest of us up."

What a sad and silly argument. How long are black people going to wait for restitution? Here's a hint: "It's not coming! So, pull your own damned self up! Get out of the basket and leave the crab, lobster, and other seafood there.

Scene: TWO FRIENDS—ONE BECOMING, ONE WITHERING

SAMUEL: It really is important to try to achieve as much as

possible and not interact with people who are satisfied with what they have.

WILLIE: Hey man! You're a nigger, just like me. So don't try to act like you're better than everybody.

SAMUEL: Well, I am like you in terms of skin color and some shared history, but there are a lot of ways you and I are different.

WILLIE: Nigger, you're lost. You better get hip to what's happening and stop talking all that smack.

5

Free at Last, Free at Last

To keep our faces toward change and behave
like free spirits in the presence of fate is strength
undefeatable.

—Helen Keller
Let Us Have Faith

Scene: SUNDAY MORNING AT FIRST CORINTHIANS CHURCH,
THIRD PEW

CHOIR [*singing and swaying*]:
We shall overc-o-m-e.
We shall overc-o-m-e.
We shall overcome, some day-ay-ay-ay-ay.
Oh, oh, deep in my heart, I do believe
We shall overcome someday.

GRANDMOTHER: Amen! Amen! Wasn't that nice, baby?

GRANDSON: Yes, Grandma. It was nice.

[*Grandmother continues to hum the tune*]

GRANDMOTHER [*tears welling in her eyes*]: You know boy,
they're telling the truth. Deep in my heart, I *do* believe,
we shall overcome someday. Do you understand that,
son?

35

GRANDSON: I think so, Grandma. [*Pause*] Grandma, I don't
understand why some people have so much, and people
like us don't have nothing.

MOTHER: Boy, if you don't be quiet . . .

GRANDMOTHER [*to daughter*]: It's okay. [*To grandson*] Well,
baby, it's God's way. But that's okay. [*Grandmother
flashes big smile to grandson*] This world don't mean a
thing. We will overcome! Things will be better in that
upper room.

As a youngster I thought, Yeah. One day we'll have what
others have. Just like Grandma says, "We'll all be the same
in the afterlife." But as I grew up and my perspectives
changed, I thought, What the hell is wrong with things
being better in *this life*? Unfortunately, in many black communities the watchword has traditionally been postponement. Many black persons are frightened by the prospect
of defeat or inadequacy in the face of the system. They wait
for the system to provide its benefits to them. Or they await
some indeterminate future when their economic lot will
have improved. Miscalculating, they wait.

Postponing one's desires and aspirations to some day
eons on or to the next life is a habit that needs to be broken.
Such practices usually constrict the motivation to succeed.
As a consequence, people are likely to accept the domi-
nance of *the system* and its supposed limitations upon
their lives. They are less apt to strive for a better life since,
as Grandma insisted, "This world don't mean a thing."

For black people, this obeisance has been passed from
generation to generation, creating legions of dysfunctional,
unmotivated, impotent persons. Many black people believe
that *the system* makes high achievement unattainable for
them. You can see them "hanging out" every day in our
cities—hundreds and thousands of losers, retired from life.
Many of them have assumed that there is little need to try
to succeed when success means so little in this world. For
them it becomes permissible, if not customary, to eschew

competing for position in the pluralistic society.[1] Believing themselves excluded from normal economic and social discourse, many simply accept the fate that they have concluded or been taught befalls them.

Directly and indirectly, black children are instructed about the "unassailable" obstacles to their success in the pluralistic world. From the observation and admonitions of their role models, children learn to shrink at the prospect of challenging the "undefeatable" obstacles before them. As well, black folklore regarding the legacies of slavery serves to confirm further the power and endurance of these obstacles. To their detriment, children are schooled in the considerable injustices prepared to thwart them. Among these obstacles are prejudice, racism, and discrimination—the Big Three.

These obstacles appear particularly unassailable when one considers that many black persons have inherited little from their parents on which to build. Without benefit of a strong economic or success foundation, many blacks find themselves battling against a ghetto mentality that inhibits the thinking and aspirations of its inhabitants. While these persons establish achievement orientations for themselves and their families, they fight the characteristic tendency to give up, which abounds in ghetto mentality. Others find themselves rationalizing or offering excuses for lack of success in black communities. They choose to accept the omnipotence of the Big Three and become apologists[2] for their own ineffectuality as well as that of their race peers.

---

1. *Pluralism*, as defined by *Funk & Wagnall's Standard Dictionary*, suggests a social condition in which disparate religious, ethnic, and racial groups are part of a common community.

2. The term *apologist* is employed to describe those persons who offer excuses or rationalizations for the circumstances in which black people find themselves. Typically, apologists hinge their arguments of disparities between black persons and white persons upon prejudice, racism, and discrimination: the Big Three. Apologists, rather reflexively, invoke the Big Three as mitigators whenever anyone suggests that black persons take responsibility for their social and economic conditions.

Apologists argue that those black persons who want to better themselves often are not able to do so under the burden of inherited economic deficit. They argue that many black persons are caught in an unending pattern of simply ensuring their weekly (sometimes daily) survival. Further, they postulate that the urgency of subsistence pre-empts any efforts toward economic stability. Purportedly prejudice, racism, and discrimination are the mechanisms that perpetuate the economic bondage of black people. Apologists conclude that black people are, indeed, still enslaved, still subject to the machinations of white society.

Some people, particularly those entrapped in black rhet-oric, would assert that slavery still exists today, embodied in prejudice, racism, and discrimination. These apologists mistakenly suggest that the chains of enslavement and oppression are still present—invisible—but just as binding. They cite inferior schools and education, job and housing discrimination, police abuse, and societal and institutional racism as the present-day chains that enslave black people. They argue, with unshakable resolve, that black people continually have to face enormous and often insurmount-able obstacles to obtain the same opportunities as their age peers.

Slavery probably does exist in some fashion, but the enslavers are *ourselves*. It is *ourselves* we need to over-come! We need to defeat those ideas of the system as evil monster or benevolent parent. We need to demolish those ideas that cast us as pawns of the system. Arguments that offer such excuses only reinforce ideas of powerlessness in segments of black communities. These arguments release those purportedly poor, downtrodden, enslaved people of their obligation to strive—and better themselves. These arguments are dangerous because any persons who have had little history of economic and social success may, likely, relish the opportunity to externalize responsibility for personal failure. They can simply reference their lack of success to the Big Three, while they await equality, liberty, and compensation for past injustices.

Those who wait for the United States government and citizenry to live up to their credo are actually colluding with the system they abhor. By waiting, one becomes guilty of failing to challenge the system. The system might or might not free us from the effects of slavery or the Big Three. But, by waiting, we foster dependence upon the system. We do not move forward. We remain mired in the same position, awaiting rescue by some savior (the government, God, the welfare system, or some other similar parenting figure). We are left to sing "We Shall Overcome."

In the era of legalized slavery, a philosophy of postponement and acquiescence may have functioned to deflect the wrath of the enslavers. A slave's industry and zealousness could be rewarded with punishment, torture, and death. At present there exists no legalized slavery; therefore, accepting the postponement philosophy has become obsolete.

Moreover, the histories of black people run counter to the excuses and rationalizations of apologists. There have always been those people who have resisted (covertly and overtly) oppression, whether it emanated from within the system or from within themselves. These resisters have included runaway slaves, saboteurs, civil rights activists of all ethnicities, Quakers and other whites, and even foreign governments. Shamefully there have also been those persons who have *not* met the challenges of our ancestors. They have chosen to acquiesce to the system. They have relented.

Many people—black, white, others—have been beaten, disgraced, raped, and killed in their efforts to gain or support the rights that accompany freedom. Black people have a responsibility to themselves and to those who have suffered and sacrificed to further the practices of freedom. That responsibility includes not enslaving ourselves. Through philosophies that embrace the insurmountability of prejudice, racism, and discrimination we enslave ourselves. Reticence and inaction toward prejudice, racism, and discrimination help to enslave us. Acceptance of one's economic lot as a *faît accompli* helps to enslave us. Rather than hanging on to the familiarity of the chains—waiting to be freed—free yourself. The system provides the chains, but only we as individuals can clamp them shut.

Just for argument's sake, let's assume that the Big Three are present as unconquerable foes. That is, "the system" is stacked mightily against black people. Given this assumption, it would seem obvious that part of the battle toward freedom and success must be waged by all black people against this system. After all, this assumption would suggest that the system operates to the disadvantage of *all* black persons. However, there are troublesome inconsistencies with such an assumption. Most notably, prejudice, racism, and discrimination do not similarly affect all black persons. We do not all enjoy equal opportunities for success or failure. One's probability of experiencing success or failure is affected by more than prejudice, racism, and discrimination. For example, individual attributes such as personal abilities, motivations, reinforcement histories, and perspectives about freedom and success also affect one's economic and social outcomes.

The importance of these attributes cannot be overstated. They affect our sense of the world and our effectiveness in it. For example, many people still operate with an outdated and outmoded perspective on race relations. These anachronauts[3] believe the world is still separated into black and white. They still contend that much of what happens to the advantage or disadvantage of people is a function of race. This "retrospective" has been taught to generations of black people. And those affected, true to their teachings, have permitted societal, economic, and political changes to pass them by.

---

3. Anachronauts in that their thinking is characteristically antiquated and old-fashioned, dysfunctional for present times.

Anachronauts, however, are in error. There are many black persons who enjoy considerable success, as there are many nonblack persons who experience considerable failure. For those trapped in black rhetoric, it must be quite threatening to consider that the reason for people's lack of success lies largely within themselves. Blame is always easier to externalize than to internalize. Most people would rather blame others than themselves for their chronic difficulties. When such blaming occurs on an individual level, it is unfortunate. But when it exists on a community level, it is a deathknell for those lacking the strength to forge ahead unreinforced and castigated by the community.

Anachronauts must, for reasons of tradition, identity, and self-perception, sing the blues of the Big Three. It is a song they know and have practiced well. Interestingly, they are threatened not only by prejudiced, racist, and discriminating white persons but also by black persons who do not buy into their philosophies. The latter group represents a particularly threatening challenge to anachronauts' world view. Such blacks undoubtedly compromise anachronauts' ability to complain categorically on behalf of all black people. Successful black persons have "made it" in a world that is, as propagated by anachronauts, against them.

Anachronauts are usually able to reconcile this inconsistency by suggesting that these "few" success stories are not success stories at all. They believe these successes to be anomalies and, as such, not replicable by the majority of black persons. They must believe this is the case, because by definition, anachronauts spend much time complaining about past problems affecting the present aspirations of black people. They often try to enjoin their peers to behave and think accordingly. Alternatively they suggest that successful black persons have "sold out," are Uncle Toms, or are trying to be white.

There are, no doubt, increasing numbers of success stories among black people. (However, these successes do not mean that humans have overcome their foibles about racial differences. No, we, as a species, remain primitive enough to hold tenaciously to those prejudices that we purport differentiate us by race.) These success stories suggest that with the correct preparation (that is, motivation, education or training, and perseverance) *all* people may enjoy success. As evidenced by the increasing number and variety of fields where black persons are present, race as a determinant of success is decreasing. *Yes*, accept it. Despite people's periodic attempts to revive and recapture the familiar misunderstandings and difficulties among racial groups, race continues to have decreasing influence upon upward mobility for those persons who are sufficiently motivated, educated, and/or trained.

In order for us to become *free at last*, we must be willing to throw off *all* the chains of oppression. Some of these chains are from the larger society and its historical treatment of black people. We all know these irons well. But there are other chains. There are those chains that come from ourselves. We have to truly believe in our individual ability to be successful in *this* society. Despite self-doubt and self-defeating attitudes, we must transcend internal limitations and control our destinies.

Still other chains come from our formative communities. Through the reinforcement of attitudes of entitlement and through acquiescence to the Big Three, our communities chain us to a limited world perspective.

Break free!

6 _____

Forces That Impinge Upon Freedom and Success

> An obstacle is something you see when you take your eyes off the goal.
>
> —West African saying

The process of becoming successful is much more than simply a matter of race. It involves at least three interdependent forces that singly or in concert may differentiate success from failure: *the system*, *the personal*, and *the cultural*. Systems and cultures affect our sense of our own potential, and our personal actions affect how systems and cultures react to us. Each of us may be constricted in our efforts toward freedom and success by *any* of these three forces. Each can have profound effects upon the probability of our success.

The system force. The effects of the system have been written about comprehensively. Institutional racism and discrimination, fewer job opportunities, and differing access to paths of success are but a small sample of the system's influence. The reportedly debilitating effects of the system seem obvious to many people. With astounding dispatch and regularity, the injustices of the system are pleaded by its purported victims. So automatic is the tendency to malign the system that rarely does anyone consider the contribution of other forces to the debilitation of individuals.

The culture-of-origin force. Less often written about, but probably presenting more impediments, is the *culture-of-origin*[1] force. It is essential to distinguish between culture of origin and other cultures. The notion of culture of origin is similar to what sociologists term *ascribed status*, that is, the status to which we are born. The cultures to which we gain membership through our efforts are conceptually similar to the term *achieved status*.

Our cultures of origin may have profound effects upon our perspective of the system and of ourselves. For example, if an individual's culture of origin reinforces hard work and perseverance, then the individual is likely to work hard, persevere, and enjoy freedom and success. If, however, an individual's culture of origin is malevolent, blaming, accusational, and acrimonious, then the individual is likely to emulate these characteristics and abjure the struggle toward freedom and success.

People commonly assume that culture is largely defined by race, gender, and socioeconomic status. The notion that people must be born, live, and die as members of one culture is a dangerous one. It is suggestive of a caste system in which one is irrevocably tied to a group by birth (for example, by reason of race). At one time in United States history consideration of black people as a caste was socioeconomically expedient. But at present such casting is without sociological, cultural, or moral foundation.

Race is *not* culture. Even what is popularized as *black culture* is contested by the many and varied individuals

1. Culture of origin refers to one's culture of birth. Although genetics (e.g., race, gender) has traditionally and monstrously been used as a major criterion for culture of origin, other variables (e.g., socioeconomic status, religion) more accurately define this sociological construct.

who make up this racial group. For example, as a result of their different perspectives, black ghetto dwellers, who value education, are culturally different from those black ghetto dwellers who value criminality. The former group is likely to foster an environment where education and educational attainment are important. The latter group is likely to identify other values to reinforce.

People are not unalterably tied to the cultures to which they are born. As individuals achieve and develop, they gain access to myriad cultures. Traditionally, people born in black ghettos have considered the ghetto to be their culture of origin *and* of lifelong membership. However, in actuality, people traverse and maneuver from culture to culture. Black persons, for example, may become artisans, or historians, or travel agents, or drug lords. All these fields constitute specific cultures; cultures to which all qualified persons will be afforded membership. One is not tied to these cultures by race. Race does not define culture; generationally transmitted ways of living do. Cultures are permeable.

THE PERSONAL FORCE

Both the *system* and *culture of origin* may have positive and negative effects upon people. An individual's likelihood of enjoying freedom and success is a function of both system and culture-of-origin forces. These forces operate to bet or thwart individuals' inputs and outcomes. To blame "the system" solely for one's recurrent failures or for others' success seriously ignores or underestimates the more significant influence of the culture-of-origin force.

Let's take the example of Andrew—a black child growing up in the United States. As Andrew matures toward responsible interaction within the society, he will be forced to fight a number of battles. In order to become more than is normally expected of him, Andrew will have to wage a battle with *the system*. This may entail extra study in order to demonstrate his competencies. He will also have to learn to negotiate effectively the barriers erected through the Big Three. These behaviors will likely help him demonstrate his readiness to interact within the system.

Andrew will also have to wage *personal* battles. He will have to learn to resist any self-defeating proclivities within his own character. One of these proclivities relates to the system's effects upon him. That is, have the supposed effects of the Big Three compromised his perspective of his abilities and opportunities for success? Has he come to believe his abilities and opportunities are thwarted by *the system*—traditionally personified as "the white man"? Does he believe that he truly cannot compete? Has he begun to limit himself? Have these doubts become integrated into his self-concept? All these considerations are part of his *personal* battle.

Scene: THREE STUDENTS IN DORMITORY ROOM AT THE STATE UNIVERSITY

STEVEN: Man, sometimes I think I'm just wasting my time. I go to school every damned day and study and pretend that I'm learning something. For what? All I need to learn to be a black man in this country is back on the corner.

DONALD: I know what you mean. No respect from the white man. And by being here, I'm losing respect on the street. [*Pause*] This environment is so artificial. They'll call me "white boy" when I graduate. I know them niggers.

STEVEN: And check this out. It doesn't matter. There's plenty of brothers out there with college degrees who still can't find a gig. You gotta be white to get ahead in this world. [*Pause*] Like, remember Reggie? He dropped out, went back to his boys, and is supposed to be driving a BMW *right now* while we sit up here in this stupid room.

DONALD: That's all the white men will give us: the ghetto. We can be kings there, but try to break into the white world and see how much a king you'll be.

PAUL [*irritated*]: I'm tired of you niggahs talking all this shit. You can be whatever you want to be if you get your head straight and get off your black ass.

DONALD [*shocked*]: Man, what are you talking about? White folks control it no matter where you go. I'm from Philadelphia, and Steve's from New York. It's the same shit wherever you go.

PAUL: I'm talking about you. Yeah, the white man controls a lot, but you're letting him control your mind. [*Pause*] And you're one of the smarter brothers on campus. Decide what you want and then go for it.

STEVEN [*just above a whisper*]: Hmm. Nigger's crazy.

PAUL: Hey, man, I'm not tripping; you are. If you take your ass back to the ghetto, what you gonna get? Niggahs robbing niggahs, niggahs killing niggahs. There ain't nothing in the street but heartache, brothers.

DONALD: Yeah, but this world is breaking my heart too.

In order to wage the personal battle, one has to first *believe* that there is a battle within oneself to fight. That is, that there are some aspects of the progress toward freedom and success which are very much under one's control. Andrew must be willing to take responsibility for his inputs and his outcomes. However, black people have been unabashedly taught to believe that the system/the government/the white man is the root of their problems. The argument goes, "If the system/the government/the white man would only live up to their creed and people weren't racist, then we could become or own or do whatever we want." We are taught that it is not we who are responsible for our fates, but some external force that is responsible for the past, present, and future of black people. Self-sufficiency is not stressed enough in the struggle to overcome. We need to be able to affect positively those personal attributes (for example, toil and perseverance) that help us, as individuals, to overcome.

It will be difficult and quite threatening for many persons to believe that they, individually, are largely responsible for their lot. For them, much too much energy has gone into a blaming mode, while not nearly enough energy has gone into an achieving mode. Rather than pursuing goals that would usher them into legitimate and promising spheres, many people expend their efforts in blaming external sources (for example, the white man or the Big Three) for their present conditions. Thereby they maintain and bequeath to their children the teachings of failure. Consequently many black persons have not enjoyed success in the pluralistic world but only in alternate, nefarious activity. Or, as dysfunctional, they become adept at the self-delusion of powerlessness. It is indeed a delusion because it's not *the white man* who steals your future; it's you.

Imagine the limitedness of all those who consider "the white man" the personification of all the despair, problems, failures, and difficulties they experience. Such persons are shackled by their defeatist perspective of the world. By externalizing problems (i.e., blaming others), individuals may protect their own self-esteem. "After all," they rationalize, "it's the system/the government/the white man who limits me, not myself." By subscribing to such perspectives, individuals need not try to improve themselves because, in their minds, all the cards are already stacked against them. In reality, however, there are potentially only three cards stacked against any person: a *system* card, a *personal* card, and a *culture-of-origin* card. And, much as in a three-on-one basketball game, most of the time the one will be beaten by the three. But individuals can increase the odds of winning (success) by decreasing the power or influence of self-limiting personal behavior (the personal card) as well as the influence of cultural constraints (the culture-of-origin card).[2] A victory over personal and cultural constraints will strengthen you immea-

2. Change also needs to be effected on the larger system (the system card). However, it's too large and distant a goal to attain in one lifetime.

surably for the battle with the system. Minus personal and cultural constraints, an individual may move toward the creation of a one-on-one situation; *you* against *the system*. Serendipitously, as black persons thrust off the limiting effects of personal and cultural constraints, the system is likely to provide access for them, at least on an individual basis.

This Model Toward Success and Freedom does not dismiss the effects of the Big Three. It suggests not only a recognition of the undeniable influence of prejudice, racism, and discrimination upon blacks' (especially ghetto dwellers') psyches, but also the recognition that self-limiting and self-oppressing attitudes contribute to the lack of freedom and success in significant segments of black communities. These attitudes constitute an increasingly large part of the culture-of-origin force. In many segments of black communities, the defeatist perspective of the individual is reinforced communally. Hence, living in such a situation, Andrew would have to wage battles with the personal force as well as with the culture-of-origin force. It is not uncommon to hear persons remark, "The white man is keeping us down." "A brother or sister can never get ahead because it's all part of "the man's game." "It's a white world"—[Intimating that there is little that a black person can do to enjoy success in "the white world".

Whose world it is seems a debatable point. Even if one could demonstrate, irrefutably, that the world is "a white man's world," so what? One must decide whether this is a point of any significance and, more important, if that should limit one's efforts and achievements. Of course, one may have to put forth more effort and endure more trials than one's peers from other groups, but the struggle should be worth the effort. One must, at minimum, try to achieve, try to succeed, dare to challenge. To do otherwise is to self-limit and self-oppress.

For Andrew, the culture-of-origin battle should be waged initially by interacting with those of similar ilk; those individuals who are endeavoring to achieve and succeed. He should learn to examine critically the supposed impediments that many black people decry. One crucial question for Andrew will be, "Are these much-discussed impediments truly omnipotent hindrances or simply omnipresent excuses?"

Succumbing to *any* impediment constitutes a negation and rejection of the struggles and pains in the histories of black people. People have sacrificed, fought, and died so that some part of the community may do better than preceding generations. How dare anyone, through inactivity, reticence, or resignation, taint the efforts of those ancestors?

> Well, son, I'll tell you:
> Life for me ain't been no crystal stair.
> It's had tacks in it,
> And splinters,
> And boards torn up,
> And places with no carpet on the floor—
> Bare.
> But all the time
> I'se been a-climbin' on,
> And reachin' landin's,
> And turnin corners,
> And sometimes goin' in the dark
> Where there ain't been no light.
> So boy, don't you turn back.
> Don't you set down on the steps
> 'Cause you find it's kinder hard.
> Don't you fall now—
> For I'se still goin', honey,
> I'se still climbin',
> And life for me ain't been no crystal stair.
> —LANGSTON HUGHES, *Mother to Son*

Again, the model toward Success and Freedom does not

cast as inconsequential the effects of the Big Three. It is crucially important to recognize their effects, and, given these effects, to plan and pursue a course of action that is proactive and not defeatist. Otherwise we resign ourselves to present conditions. We relent to that which is perceived and taught as our fate. We communicate to our children that we, as a people, shall overcome *someday*, while not urging ourselves to overcome *today*. It's time to stop singing those damned songs. Let's not wait for the larger society and the world to give us freedoms and opportunities. Let's take a hint from the previous 350 years of United States history in the treatment of black people.

It seems to me imperative that black people begin to live with eyes cast toward the future, rather than bolstering and wallowing in past, separatist, and blame-placing philosophies. Let's dare to be bold, innovative, achievement- and success-oriented, future- and pluralistic-minded. Take your destiny into your own hands, rather than continuing to hold hands with dysfunctional philosophies and teachings that emanate from one's culture of origin.

Scene: TWO BROTHERS ON A STREET CORNER

JOE: Yo! Bobby! Where you been? Ain't seen you in a long time.

ABDUL: Hey man, I told you I no longer use the blue-eyed devil's name. My name is now Abdul.

JOE: Well, Abdul, where you been?

ABDUL: I went to the motherland.

JOE: To where?

ABDUL: The motherland, my brother. To Africa.

JOE: For what?

ABDUL: To commune with our African brothers and sisters. Black people! You see, my brother, in order for us all to know ourselves we must discover our African heritage.

JOE: Gonna tell me some more of that Africa shit, Bobby? I mean Abdul.

ABDUL: You see, my brother, the white man has messed up

your mind. All black people, all over the world, need to reunite with their African roots. Be proud of your African heritage.

JOE: Bobby, this isn't Africa. This is North Philly.

ABDUL: Man, if you would just listen to my message I would educate you of the white man's theft of your African heritage. The devil has tricked us. It's all part of his plan. Do you have time to hear? Do you have time to hear of the legacy and your destiny?

JOE: Maybe tomorrow, Abdul. Maybe tomorrow.

A Case in point. Let's look at an example where the culture-of-origin force comes to bear upon individuals' probabilities of experiencing freedom and success. A child-hood playmate of mine became pregnant and had her first baby at age thirteen. Although disconcerting, such an oc-currence was not unusual in my community of origin. More interesting was that my playmate's mother had birthed her at age fourteen, and so, too, with her mother before her. When my playmate's child, a girl, turned four-teen, she had her first baby. Her eighteen-year-old boy-friend was welcomed, with open arms, into the family.

In this family there were four generations of females who gave birth soon after they reached puberty. As one can readily surmise, none of these children born to teenage mothers had a good opportunity to be much more than a link in this chain. One could blame institutional racism, discrimination, unresponsive social services, poor school-ing, "the white man," ad infinitum. However, a more accu-rate assessment would have to place a large part of the responsibility on this particular family's structure, norms, values, and beliefs. Moreover, in communities where there exist attitudes of acquiescence and capitulation, one is likely to be faced with escalating rates of teenage pregnan-cy, undereducation, joblessness, criminality, and drug abuse.

Although the above example may be extreme, it highlights some concerns. That is, what are the community or family legacies that impede one's progress? What dysfunctional perspectives and philosophies do we pass on to our children and peers? What are the personal and cultural legacies and philosophies that serve to compromise freedom and success for black people? Perhaps some of yours are listed below.

Racism is much too difficult to fight.
Prejudice is much too difficult to fight.
Discrimination is much too difficult to fight.
Don't become an Uncle Tom/Aunt Sally.
The white man is against us.
Schools are terrible.
Selling out.
Don't lose your ethnic heritage.
Be black.
Black people can't get anywhere in the white man's world.
You have to be white to get ahead in this world.
Niggers ain't shit.
Black people are always going to be down.
Don't try to be white.
It's not my fault; it's white people who have caused this.
White folks owe us a debt.

So strong are mythology and folklore in black communities that they are often accepted uncritically. Many individuals become incensed and seethe at even an intimation that one would question the veracity of hallowed and consecrated beliefs. These personal and cultural legacies are maintained with a ferocity that is astounding and tragically, they only serve to obscure our children's view of the future. In effect, we are aborting any hope for successive generations to change existing conditions in black communities.

7

Theoretical Considerations for Why Mythology Is Maintained in Black Communities

> A belief is not merely an idea the mind possesses; it is an idea that possesses the mind.
> —Robert Bolton

Despite the level of education, increased cultural sensitivity, and common sense, myths remain woven into our social fabric. Defying logic, rationality, and statistics, people continue to maintain these myths. From a psychosocial perspective, a number of theories may account for the persistence of such myths in our daily lives. These theories attempt to explain how humans cognitively acquire, process, and maintain information. They may also account for the resistance of myths, beliefs, and values to change.

Schemata. One theory suggests that it is quite impossible to manage all the information present in our daily interactions. So many different types of people and situations are presented to us that we are easily overwhelmed by the myriad levels of communication necessary to negotiate through our daily lives. The process of social interaction would be greatly retarded if we attempted to treat, without some use of preconceived notions, each person as an individual. We would have to take the time to assess each one and form an individual impression.

Although individualized and nonprejudiced social interaction is socially desirable, it can be extremely time-consuming. In the interests of efficiency, humans employ relatively stable cognitive patterns or schemata[1] for interpreting the enormous amount of information encountered daily. Schemata function as a type of cognitive shorthand, permitting us to engage in our daily lives without being overwhelmed by the complexities of the world. Through the use of schemata, we may reduce the amount of information encountered to a level which is, so to speak, digestible for our brains.

We have all witnessed the manifestation of schema in childhood. Let's assume a little girl, Sarah, has a dog at home. She calls it "Doggie." On a visit to the local zoo, Sarah sees a tiger and a lion and an ocelot. What is she likely to call each of these animals? At a certain age, Sarah will call each of these animals "Doggie." With a limited number of categories from which to draw, she has yet to learn the distinctions among animals. She is demonstrating a restricted schema for four-footed animals. Sarah incorporates all such creatures into her "Doggie" schema.

Adults may also manifest mental patterns through which they organize the world. These patterns are relatively inflexible, but general ways of negotiating the environment.

---

1. The term *schema* (pl., *schemata*) was first popularized through the theories of Jean Piaget. His critically influential theory suggests that schemata are the primary mental patterns or elements through which an infant first organizes the environment. For example, a child who is a few weeks of age organizes the world orally. Through sucking, she comes to know the environment which affects her.

Schema is to be distinguished from stereotype in that the latter is invoked specific to particular groups, while the former is a generalized mental pattern.

For example, an individual who is apprehensive of all who are different form himself manifests a schema characterized by xenophobia. With little variation, his interactions will be defined by the criterion of similarity/dissimilarity. He will evaluate others by this criterion and organize his world accordingly.

Adults may also be motivated to lessen the number of categories to which they must attend. By treating certain visible characteristics (for example, race, ethnicity, gender, or even attire) as diagnostic constants, adults may reduce the amount of time and effort expended in social interaction. Such treatment will result in seemingly efficient negotiation of our daily lives. Just as Sarah has a schema for "Doggie," adults may have stereotypes for blacks, whites, gays, males, females, people in business suits, etcetera. That is, we permit ourselves to view all blacks, whites, gays, males, females, or persons in business suits as fairly invariable, thereby reducing the complexity of our lives. We need not consider the idiosyncrasies of individuals. We can simply define them as members of those groups whose fixed behaviors, attitudes, and values we have already settled upon. Schemata underlie stereotypes.

Albeit expedient, the use of schemata to process the world is troublesome when applied indiscriminately in all social spheres. There are, for example, significant ramifications for invariant sexism or racism. Since adults are usually more sophisticated than children, we are usually more able to monitor our own behavior appropriately. However, our underlying cognitive structure remains that of a restricted schema. This may account for how certain attitudes become entrenched in psyches. For example, prejudice (an attitudinal manifestation of schemata) is much more difficult to modify than discrimination (a behavioral manifestation of schemata).

Let's consider the example of Nicole, a young single female who subscribes to the myth that black males are insatiable sexual beings. Employing this myth, she is likely to react the same way to virtually all black males, regardless of their individual differences. She will not recognize or attend to those black males who do not fit her stereotype. The existence of such "rarities" challenge her and threaten to alter the perspective of the world that has become most familiar and comfortable for her. Thus she discounts the challenges represented by any "rare" black males and treats them as aberrations. She is thereby able to retain her mental pattern and negotiate the world's complexities with a simple-minded facility. Schemata can be very powerful and central aspects of the way we process the world.

When we are forced to face an example that does not fit our schema or stereotype, we may find ourselves confused. Let's assume that Nicole encounters a black male who is uninterested in her sexually. According to the theory, there are two ways she can address the discrepancy between this man's behavior and the information she has always assumed to be true. The first process is termed *assimilation*. Through this process she may absorb the discrepant example into her existing schema by ignoring or minimizing the discrepancy. For example, Nicole may conclude that the uninterested man is not a *real, true* black man or that he is simply more cunning than the usual man. Irrespective of her choice, she does not relinquish her schema for black males. As a result, she is able to maintain her stereotype.

Alternatively, but probably less likely, she may employ a process termed *accommodation*. Through this process she may expand her existing mental structure by appending the discrepant example to her existing schema. In Nicole's case, she would have to conclude she has been short-sighted and that there are more facets to black males than the purely sexual. She would thereby accept and respect the differences among black males.

For children, the processes of assimilation and accommodation are crucial in helping them come to know and negotiate the world. Assimilation and accommodation serve to expand and refine their world view. For adults, too, these processes may be used similarly or differently to maintain a restricted, but familiar, view of the world.

The processes of assimilation and accommodation underlie prejudice. For instance, an individual who is steeped in a sexist tradition will likely maintain his perspective (schema) through an overutilization of assimilation and an underutilization of accommodation. Similarly, people may maintain their myths about black male behavior by differentially employing accommodation and assimilation.

Confirmatory and disconfirmatory information. Another theory that explains the resistance of myth to logic, rationality, and statistics suggests that humans give differential weight to information that confirms or disconfirms their schema. Confirming evidence is weighted more heavily. That is, information that is consistent with our world view, our biases, has a more pronounced effect upon us than does evidence that is inconsistent with that world view.

Each Thursday, after her evening class, Nicole rides the subway home. One evening she notices a young black man repeatedly glancing at her. He seems to be looking at her legs. She tries to ignore him, but, to her terror, he approaches. Dependent upon what transpires, her myth for black males ("They are all insatiable sexual beings") may be affected. If she is faced with information that confirms her myth—the young man says, "Hey, baby. What's your name? Damn, you're looking good tonight. I'd like to be your man for a few hours,"—she is likely to retain her stereotype. If, however, she is faced with information that disconfirms her myth, the young man bends over, picks up a five-dollar-bill and says, "Excuse me, miss. I think you dropped this." He then hands the money to her and returns to his seat. She is likely to experience confusion at this challenge to her stereotype. She must somehow reconcile this discrepant information. She *may* adjust her schema to incorporate this disconforming information, but most likely her biases (schemata, myths, stereotypes) will remain firmly intact and entrenched through the differential use of confirming and disconfirming evidence. The former situation not only serves as confirmation, but fortifies her stereotype as a correct and justified one. In the latter situation, she is likely to discount this man's behavior as unrepresentative.

Selection bias. Selection bias is still another considera-tion in the maintenance of myth. This theory posits that the persons we choose as representative of a group are usually those that reflect our biases. All examples that would challenge our biases or schemata are discounted. We rarely consider those persons who do not fit our per-sonal schema. For Nicole, she will likely consider as proto-typical only those men who reflect her schema, while ig-noring those men who do not. This selectivity enables her to maintain her schema.

Thus, on the following Thursday evening when she is leered at by a group of black males, her selection bias will emerge. She will likely view their behavior as typical and representative of black males, while ignoring the behavior of those black men who do not accost her or even those who may come to her aid.

Statistical theory. Statistical theory offers another expla-nation for why myths, once formed, are resistant to mod-ification. Toward efficient processing of information from the environment, people may employ a strategy that re-duces the multifariousness of a group. When dealing with large groups of people, it seems expedient to employ a "cognitive mean": an intuitive average that presumably is representative of large groups of people. Through the use of this statistical concept a person need not encounter, separately, each member of a group. Rather that person can observe (or worse, hear of) the behavior of a few group members and form an impression of what is "typical" for the group. Thus, instead of having to engage each member of a group individually in order to form an impression, an "average" is utilized. From conjecture, presumption, or repeated exposure to members of different groups, we may arrive at a prototype that we assume to be normative and representative.

This derived cognitive mean is our impression of accurate data about members of a group. The use of a cognitive mean is a very expedient way of dealing with the enormous amount of information generated by varied groups of people. But all too often we derive or "calculate" this mean inaccurately.

Let's look at the inaccuracies by considering, arithmetically, the computation of means. Below are two groups of scores represented by Sample A and Sample B.

Sample A	Sample B
10	4
0	6
0	6
10	6
10	4
0	4

If you add each column, you will obtain a total of thirty for both Sample A and Sample B. If you then divide each total by the number of scores in the group, you will arrive at an average (or mean) of five for Sample A and for Sample B. However, a mean of five is not equally representative of each sample. The scores of Sample B do not deviate as much from the mean of five as do the scores of Sample A. Five appears much more representative of the scores that comprise Sample B than those that comprise Sample A. This demonstrates that the computation of an arithmetic mean (or average) does not necessarily ensure the accuracy or representativeness of that mean for the samples with which one is concerned. So, too, is the case with cognitive means! Analogously, a cognitive mean does not necessarily ensure accuracy or representativeness of that mean for a group of people. Individuals from a group may deviate significantly from a cognitive mean. It would be presumptuous to make conclusions about a group of people based upon inadequate information. The consideration of the behavior of a few group members is inadequate information.

Moreover, if we take a closer look at the means of Sample A and Sample B, another interesting aspect of statistical theory becomes apparent. Although five is supposedly an accurate representation of each sample, note that *none* of the scores that are represented by the mean fall at the mean. Simply stated, although five is the "average" of each sample, there are *no* fives in either Sample A or Sample B. This same characteristic holds true for cognitive means. None of the members of a group need fall at the group mean. This is a critically important point because it suggests that averages are not necessarily typical. Averages may reflect many errors when we use them to represent any set of data or, in this case, people. Although it might be expedient to employ a cognitive mean to gauge and predict the behaviors and attitudes of others, none of these "others" need reflect that average.

The basic assumption underlying a cognitive mean (as with any mean) is its representativeness of normative information about a sample (group). People seem to ignore or, at best, underutilize information from examples that do not fit their cognitive mean. As with scores, individuals who do not fall at the mean also reflect very important information about the variability of a group. Without consideration of all group members, one is unable to appreciate the range of characteristics for a group. This lack of appreciation of the range of a group is the quintessence of racism. Racist individuals do not recognize the range of characteristics for individuals who comprise a group.

Through the employment of schemata, differential use of confirming and disconfirming evidence, selection bias, and

cognitive means people are able to maintain and perpetuate myths and folklore.

Let's consider an example in which all these factors
interplay to maintain myth. George, an auto mechanic, has
always treated women equally; as sexual objects and potential sexual conquests. He, like his father, has never re-
spected any woman. In fact, he believes that all females
should remain in the home. He has said that "All a professional woman needs to make her a *real* woman is a good
man." Furthermore, he insists that every woman wants a
man to control her.

As George arrives at work one morning, he is introduced
to a new, reportedly highly trained and competent mechanic, a woman. During her first few days on the job, the
quality of her work equals or exceeds the work level of the
male mechanics. However, on that Friday at the end of
the shift, George finds her in a back room crying due to the
harassment the guys have heaped upon her.

George has been presented with information that challenges his myths. There are a number of ways George may
respond to this challenging information. He may assimilate
the information by questioning her femaleness ("She's really more man than woman") or suspecting her motivations
("She's really looking for a husband"). Alternatively, he may
accommodate the information by admitting his erroneous
assumptions ("I guess I was wrong. A woman can be as
competent as any man"). George could maintain and bol-
ster his myth by underutilizing the disconfirming evidence
("Anybody could do the work she's been assigned to do"),
while overutilizing the confirming evidence ("Just like all
women, when things get tough she cries").

These cognitive processes, together or singly, can act to
foster, maintain, and perpetuate myth. So too, these processes operate in the maintenance and perpetuation of
myth in black communities. If we are motivated to believe
that white persons are against us, there will be little difficulty in maintaining our myth. Through the differential use

of assimilation and accommodation, confirming and disconfirming evidence, selection bias, and cognitive means, we may retain the most fiercely held myth about ourselves and others.

8

Black Mythology and Folklore: The Definition and Delineation of Blackness

> This morning when he looked at me,
> I saw how black I was
> though there was nothing I could see
> to give him any cause.
>
> But I was black all day, and mean;
> and leaving none to doubt,
> I showed all day what I had seen
> this morning stepping out.
>
> He looked me into rage and shame;
> no less, the day was grim.
> Tomorrow, by another name,
> I'll do as much for him.
> —Raymond R. Patterson, *Black All Day*

Scene: THE LOCAL SCHOOLYARD

BOBBY: Look man, when you get in the paint, look for the ball. Shit! They're laying off you, and double-teaming me.

JIM: Okay, Bobby, I'll try to get open, man. I know I missed a few last game.

BOBBY: Yeah. And relax, man. Some you missed when nobody was on you. You're playing like a white boy.
JIM: Okay, man.

I can't play hoops. Oh, I'm able to make a lay-up or two
during a game or, more rarely, hit a ten-footer. But I'm very
bad at it. I'm even worse at dribbling. So bad that a poor
player, with just a tiny bit of pressure, will cause me to pass
or lose the ball. I didn't fare much better in football. I was
an okay player in high school but never seemed to be quite
athletic enough to parlay that level of skill into a stellar
high-school experience, let alone entertain professional
career aspirations.

And since I couldn't dance or sing (as my friends and
relatives can attest) or preach, I seemingly had few legitimate avenues out of the neighborhood. At least that was
communicated to me by my role models and peers in
particular and by society in general. Indirectly and directly,
I learned that the range of careers open to blacks was
constricted. Rare was the black role model who was not an
athlete, preacher, or entertainer. These are honorable professions, and a proportionate number of youths should
aspire to them. The trouble with these aspirations is that
they are not enough. There simply needs to be a greater
array of possibilities and a less restricted view of probabilities. The dearth of role models in a wider range of
endeavor was disturbing to me then, and even now.

Contrary to popular folklore, being poor, undereducated,
unemployed, lascivious, or adept at some sport involving a
ball does not constitute a criterion for status as a righteous
and bona fide black man. Historically these criteria often
exhausted much of the range of reinforced behaviors for
black males. One shouldn't have to follow a prefabricated
life-style of "hangin' in the 'hood" and speaking a particular dialect in order to fit in with the community. However,
such racist and deliminating ideas are put forward by both
black and nonblack persons.

Some would argue that a commonality of attitudes, behaviors and values is very different when asserted by blacks than by nonblacks. Black persons, some might argue, are concerned with preservation of the culture through fostering positive and "appropriate" *black* role models for children and adults. Nonblacks may only be concerned with relegating black people to a predictable, invariant, and nonthreatening stance. However, these arguments are romanticism at best; self-delusion at worst. Even if these distinctions between black and nonblack delimiters were credible, endorsement of a common viewpoint curtails the development and advancement of black people. Constricting the range of attitudes, behaviors, and values for black people deters those persons who seek "nonsanctioned" lives. They hesitate to cross the boundaries of black conventionality, no matter who determines what that is.

Those who would cite differences between black and nonblack delimiters are most likely seeking exemption from their self-oppressive roles. It is probably less threatening for them to indict nonblack persons than to incriminate themselves for present-day circumstances.

All Americans, most desperately black people, need to recognize that the presence of blacks in myriad spheres of endeavor is advantageous not only to those who want to escape ghetto environments, but to American society in general. The number of black persons in all areas of endeavor must increase, particularly in those not traditionally reinforced in the black community. We have enough pimps, drug dealers, and other criminals. Let's increase our representation in nontraditional fields and reinforce those who choose to engage in them.

I, for one, am heartened by people who dare to buck traditions: black kids with purple, blue, yellow-dyed hair, white bands playing "black" music, black groups playing heavy metal music, people endeavoring to be lawyers, astronauts, golfers, race car drivers, ice skaters, fashion designers, ad infinitum. It's okay to deviate from the party line. Rhythm and blues is nice, but sometimes you've just got to rock and roll.

If any of us dare question the "blackness" of these sojourners, then we are indeed a very troubled group. The result of such questioning is a range of constrictive behaviors, attitudes, and cognitions. *We* are then as guilty as any other group for keeping black people *in their place*. Most persons will choose to avoid social censure rather than to contest established norms. They will opt to act, behave, believe, and think *black*. This is such a curious phenomenon. Isn't such constriction what we cry foul about when "those white people" try to limit us? Why then do we reject or castigate those black persons who dare to be groundbreakers? What are we afraid of? What scares us so much that we hold tenaciously to outmoded and dysfunctional strategies?

Although separated by regional, population, and historical differences, black communities in the United States are surprisingly similar. The ghetto in Los Angeles is not unlike the ghettoes in New York, Philadelphia, Detroit, Chicago, or Camden. In each you will find chronic and rampant underemployment, daily life-threatening events (shootings, stabbings, gang warfare), a restricted range of aspirations, and flourishing drug cultures. A sense of powerlessness in the face of economic impotence and little upward mobility characterize such communities. Most disturbing and disquieting is that these fetters are not a recent manifestation of sociopolitical and economic conditions, but enjoy a long history and boast an enduring energy.

From slavery through Jim Crow, Reconstruction, migration to the industrial North, the civil-rights era to the present, black persons have been subjected to a grossly inordinate number of indignities, rapes, beatings, and murders. In the past, these events served to lend a sense of commonality and community to black people. But, today, much of the predation on the black community comes *from* black people. To blame white people for preying on the black community ignores recent trends in the black community. The practice of attributing one's lack of mobility to racism and discrimination is antiquated and contributes to dysfunction in black communities.

The essence of upward mobility for immigrants seems to center around intergenerational success. One's great-grandfather may have been a sharecropper, his son a carpenter's assistant, his son a carpenter, and his son a shop foreman. Each successive generation is expected to do better, economically, than the previous one. However, for such a strategy to be effective it is imperative that belief in intergenerational success be shared by parents and their offspring. In the United States, resigning oneself to the same economic position as that of one's parents can bring about dependency upon the system for economic survival. Such dependence precludes upward mobility, but for many blacks it is an accepted outcome.

Black people have not historically acquiesced to a philosophy of dependence. For example, to provide for their families, many black men found themselves taking small scale or odd jobs—scufflin'—to supplement their income. The practice of scufflin' has had an important place in the struggle and histories of black men. Scufflin' is the process of doing what needs to be done to make ends meet. Scufflin' provides sustenance day to day, week to week, for one's self and family. It is self-efficacy in the face of particularly hard economic times. Collecting old newspapers and scrap metal to be sold to the junk man or working some little no-future job on the side are examples of scufflin'. Important to note, scufflin' implies legitimacy of the activity, while hustlin'—another money-generating strategy —connotes illegitimacy or shadiness.

Increasingly there are segments of black communities in which much more hustling than scuffling takes place, and where the means to economic solvency are immaterial. Each person is out for his own survival, unconcerned about fostering intergenerational mobility. Many black families and communities seem to have lost the compass of success.

There has been an obvious disruption in the process of intergenerational mobility. Perhaps the overwhelming effects of racism experienced at the hands of institutions or the reinforcing dependency of the social welfare system have derailed the process for many. Whatever the cause, the disruption has profoundly affected relations among black people. The compass of success is gravitating toward increased dependency rather than economic self-sufficiency. Worse still, many black individuals, couples, and communities are simply adrift.

I am not, in any fashion, suggesting the restricted view that *all* the problems and despair experienced by black people are caused by other blacks. Rather, I am suggesting that a significant proportion of the problems and despair experienced by many black persons does not emanate from whites. In my estimation, there exist more blacks than whites who prey on black communities. One might argue, perhaps quite persuasively, that the nature and background from which white predators and black predators operate are different. White predators may be acting to perpetuate problems and further subjugate the black community. Black predators, engaged in the same activities, may be responding to the deplorable conditions that they have experienced, and "survival" may be their goal. These arguments, however, are just excuses. For this author, predation is predation. For example, there is little justification in patronizing a shopowner of similar ethnicity who overcharges her patrons, while eschewing a competitively priced nonblack shopowner. Such practice seems silly at best, economically disastrous at worst. In the same vein, a child dead from an overdose of drugs is just as dead irrespective of the ethnicity of the dealer.

Today there exists a disorganized, undirected perspective in many segments of black communities. Rarely manifest in these segments is the structure of intergenerational mobility; at least in terms of legitimate endeavors. Role models are woefully lacking. Not only do some parents and other adults fail to provide positive role models, but many present poor examples through substance abuse and immaturity. On my travels through black communities, I have often witnessed would-be role models (females and males of all ages) purchasing drugs from those who would be their charges (children twelve to seventeen years of age).

Yes, many black persons have been compromised by historical and socioeconomic circumstances, but, more important and devastating are the self-limiting philosophies of individuals and communities, and a pervasive resignation to one's lot.

There are black people who pull down themselves and everyone around them. As long as black communities actively or passively accept these persons as members in good standing (i.e., brothers and sisters), we will remain saddled with the destruction and negative implications that accompany such individuals. This practice of ascribing brotherhood or sisterhood status is protective and may well be an outgrowth of the era of slavery and comparable shameful periods in United States history. Those times demanded community and cohesion. People needed to band together to provide mutual protection from the then legal, but immoral and capricious, actions of enslavers and detractors.

Protectionism, is dysfunctional in today's culture, and it must now be challenged from within the community. It is unconscionable to provide sanctuary to pimps, drug dealers, abusers of children, and other parasites through acquiescence, collusion, or a misguided sense of fraternity.

Protectionism has become increasingly problematic in black communities. Rather than judging people by their personality, character, or philosophical orientation, we judge them solely by race. For example, in black communities we are guilty of employing the term *brother* or *sister* indiscriminately to anyone with black skin. The definition and delineation of brotherhood/sisterhood is much too important to be treated in an unconsidered fashion, but this lesson seems to have been poorly learned. Just as there existed black persons who would divulge the secrets of slave revolts, there exist people in our communities who are destructive and otherwise not of kindred spirit.

Blackness of skin should not be an unconditional indicator of brotherhood/sisterhood. Not every person within our racial, ethnic, and geographic communities is a *brother* or a *sister*. In the past, there existed a shared oppression that has led many to assert that everyone of black skin, in each and every social and economic stratum, is a *brother* or *sister*. That is, all black persons are akin to the same victimization; all relatives of the same abused family. However, such genealogical excess is unsound, we can ill-afford to assign everyone with black skin the status of brother or sister in terms of interest in black communities as a whole. A philosophical belongingness based upon external considerations (for example, skin color, mode of dress, vernacular) is presumptuous and harmful to black people as a group. To paraphrase from a speech I heard delivered by black legislator and civil-rights leader Julian Bond, "One's relevancy cannot be measured by the length of one's hair or the intricacy of one's handshake."

There have always been individuals—trailblazers—who have departed from traditional realms of "blackness." They have refused to be limited by the horizons set for them by black people or by the larger society. They have endeavored to own businesses, reach educational goals, and they have demanded their rights when such actions were deemed impossible. It is important for black communities to reinforce these trailblazers as they expand the range of what are considered black endeavors. In our words, deeds, and aspirations we must extend our conceptions of how black is defined. Through this extension will be afforded room for those persons who have a positive (albeit nontraditional) effect upon black communities. However, those persons who have a deleterious effect upon the black community must not, through the overinclusiveness of race, be afforded its protection, lest we all be compromised through association.

I will not offer up a list of behaviors and attitudes that are representative of positive community spirit. Such a list would be reminiscent of the 1960s and 1970s when many black persons found themselves trying to "out-black" others. By joining the popular organizations of the times and/ or spouting rhetoric, they could demonstrate *their blackness* while being critical of others' *lack of blackness*. We should not return to those times. They were days characterized by repression, apprehension, and censure. (Besides, I don't own a daishiki.)

Each person in each community must arrive at some criteria by which to distinguish kindred spirits. Unfortunately, many of the distinctions that black people have employed so far are troublesome and outdated. The distinctions that many of us use often serve to separate black people by economic class, education, or associations, and not by detriment to black communities. Individuals who are financially astute, highly educated, or have white friends, are more likely to be ostracized than are those individuals who rain harm upon the community. That is, the former are tagged as Uncle Toms and sell-outs, while the latter are given the status of *brother* or *sister*.

I would not suggest a witch hunt through which people point accusingly at persons suspected of not being *with us*. I am suggesting, however, that as individuals and communities we take more care in the employment of the term *brother* or *sister*. If we indiscriminantly confer all the privileges that accompany such status, we unwittingly (perhaps subconsciously) condone the negative activities of nefarious persons in our communities. Moreover, we will continue to drive away those black persons who will not tolerate such acquiescence.

One of the more divisive areas in black communities is

socioeconomic class. Many black persons complain about what they perceive as middle-class insensitivity to their less economically solvent brethren. Many poorer persons charge that middle-class blacks have forgotten from where they came and are reluctant to help pull up others.

This is quite paradoxical since many middle-class black persons strive to remain connected to what is viewed as black communities. However, many are uncertain about the connection. One question faced by a great number of black professionals and entrepreneurs is if and how they should expose their children to "black culture." Many of my friends, acquaintances, and clients grapple with this problem, and so, I believe, do most upwardly mobile black persons. In response to this question, I point out its ambiguous nature: "What is specific to black culture?"

It is laughable to think that only poor persons comprise the black community. Such thinking is racist in itself. Worse, it is romanticism. The *poverty of black people* has become part of our folklore and therefore part of our identities. The poor black person who comes from poverty—a lineage of slaves, sharecroppers, scufflers, and welfare recipients—has become our archetype. The endorsement of this archetype does injustice to all those who have struggled *to achieve* and all those who have yet *to become*. We must stop evaluating others by this archetype. There are many well-heeled black persons who are waging battles in the larger system. Most receive little support from black communities. Yet, their presence in different spheres *is* giving back to the black communities. We need desperately to expand our ideas of what is our community and what constitutes "giving back" to it.

Regarding the exposure of black children to "black culture," there are a number of significant considerations. I want my children exposed to many varieties of valuable experience. But not all of them are exclusive or peculiar to black communities. I want my children exposed to sincere, positive, and decent persons. And I want such encounters to be with all types people of all races and genders. Since people most often choose friends due to commonality of neighborhood, school, church, or work, many black professionals will have some friends who are not black. For instance, I am a psychologist. As you may imagine most of my work acquaintances are not black. I also choose to live in a neighborhood that happens to be predominantly white. Although many of my acquaintances are white, I have friends who are black, Hispanic, Asian, and gay. We all are, to my knowledge, sincere, positive, and decent. Those are the criteria for inclusion in my world.

But, just as I feel strongly about my children's exposure to positive relationships, I am as adamant about not exposing them to the pathology that is represented in some segments of black communities. I refuse to accept into my world, in part or parcel, those aspects of black communities that are negative.

One must be critical of *all* social groups, norms, and behaviors. Using critical judgment is particularly necessary when one is asked, to accept without condition that which is "black," *because* it is black. "That's bullshit!" I will encourage and support those aspects of the community which are of merit. I will continue to veto those aspects which are not.

9

Myth and the Maligning of Black Men

I went to ma daddy,
Says Daddy I have got the blues.
Went to ma daddy
Says Daddy I have got the blues.
Ma daddy says, Honey
Can't you bring no better news?

I cried on his shoulder but
He turned his back on me.
Cried on his shoulder but
He turned his back on me.
He said a woman's cryin's
Never gonna bother me.

I wish I had wings to
Fly like the eagle flies.
Wish I had wings to
Fly like the eagle flies.
I'd fly on ma man an'
I'd scratch out both his eyes.
—Langston Hughes, *Hard Daddy*

Scene: APARTMENT 17G OF A LARGE HIGH-RISE BUILDING

PAM: Girl, I saw this fine black man on the bus yesterday.
Fine as he wanna be.
DEEDEE: How fine was he?

75

PAM: Man was so fine, make you wanna slap your momma. Had those curls, light-skinned, green eyes, everything, child!

DEEDEE: Now you know those pretty niggers will be the first ones to try to dog you out.

PAM [*Hand on hip, head bobbing back and forth, to and fro, while flashing eyelashes*]: Who you telling? I was just looking, honey. Hardly shopping.

Scene: TWO BLACK WOMEN ON THE ROUTE 23 BUS

KIM: Girl, look at them niggas on the corner. Singing. Like they're ever gonna be shit. They should be looking for a damned job.

JANICE: You know you can't depend on no black-ass nigger.

KIM: I heard that! My grandmother always said to me, "God bless the child who's got his own."

JANICE: That's right! My old man never works. He just hangs out with his buddies drinking wine and talking trash. Then he comes home smelling like some bar and want to get next to me.

KIM: Who you telling, honey? Jerome does the same shit. You can't ever get ahead with them niggas hanging around your neck like a weight, dragging your ass down.

JANICE: I hear you, girl.

Scene: TANYA AND GAIL AT WORK

GAIL: Tanya, how was your date last Friday with Gerald?

TANYA: Oh, that nigger. I thought the brother was going to be about something. But he talked the same shit all black men talk: "Baby, you look so sweet. Won't you let me take you to Chez Gerald? There we can make the sweet love together." That same trash.

GAIL: Yeah, I know. Some brother who called himself Pierre tried the same thing with me at that party last week. "Damn, baby! You're the finest thing in here. Hey, momma, why don't you and I find someplace alone where we can finish the party?" I said, "Nigger, I ain't your momma."

TANYA: And get this. Guess what Gerald does for a living. [*Pause*] The nigger drives a school bus. A damned school bus. Can you believe that? A school bus driver.

GAIL: I tell you, girl, I don't know how a sister is supposed to deal. Most of the brothers I know are in jail or junkies. And the rest don't have nothing. Just like Gerald; living from check to check.

TANYA: I want a black man who is about something. Someone with a car, a house, cute, and with a *very serious* bank account, honey. A real black man. A doctor or a lawyer, child.

GAIL: I heard that! I ain't messing with no more broke, po' men. I want a professional man. Someone who can take care of me, and give me all the shit I need. Not some brother with some piece of job who wants me to work too.

TANYA: I hear you. [*Pause*] You wanna go get some lunch?

GAIL: I can't yet. I got four more heads to do before one o'clock.

TANYA: Damn. She works us to death at this damned hairdresser.

Recently, I reread the provocative bestseller *For Colored Girls Who Have Considered Suicide / When the Rainbow Is Enuf.* I was taken with its style and verve in portraying the dilemma and enigma in which black women purport to find themselves. According to folklore, black women have striven to achieve economic, social, and political power for themselves, their families, and their communities. Supposedly, at the same time, black men have been disruptive of this achievement through irresponsibility, lethargy, and idleness. The folklore suggests that black women are saddled with the ineffectuality of their men. This myth of strong black women and weak, ineffectual black men has been celebrated in books, films, theatrical plays, and television programs. A great deal of popular black folklore bemoans the plight of black women in relation to their men.

The maligning of black men by all parties, particularly black females, enjoys a long history. The dawn of this attitude probably arose during the era of slavery, when the idea of a strong (or even responsible) black man was antithetical to the maintenance and perpetuation of that system. As a result, our ancestors were taught the myths of black male weakness, ineffectuality, slothfulness, and worthlessness. These myths have, in turn, been passed on to us all: white people, black people, everyone. They still exist, virulent, today.

Their prevalence notwithstanding, I must take exception to that most widespread of myths; that black men have little worth. This myth holds that due to their enslavement and resultant economic and social impotence, black males are inadequate to the demands of present-day living. Typically cast as incapable of responsibility for self or others, the justification for their past enslavement and present disenfranchisement evolved. There emerged the attendant myth that black women are continually and hopelessly shackled with problems caused by their men. *They* must be the saviors of the race. Purportedly it is black women who must be the vanguard for the advancement of black people, while black men exist feckless and inutile.

This myth continues to the significant detriment of black people. For black men, its endorsement fosters and reinforces a predilection toward irresponsibility, unreliability, and impotence. According to the myth, black men are rarely a part of useful and positive socioeconomic efforts; instead, they are tolerated, burdened, or assigned innocuous roles. As a result, self-sufficiency and efficacy are foreign to them. Their reinforced self-concept is that of millstones—present, but subordinate and inhibiting.

For black women, the endorsement of this myth reduces their own humanity. Rather than enjoying a cooperative, equal-status partnership with a man, a black woman is expected to be a pillar of strength; an object, with little freedom to sway from her chronicled might. Her mythical status as mother and savior of the race is both an accolade and a trap.

The purported deficits of black males are legion and are zealously enumerated in gatherings of black women. This maligning is typically passed, like folklore, from generation to generation of black women. Mothers pass to daughters, sisters to sisters, aunts to nieces. Statements such as "Never trust a black man," "They only want one thing," "They are irresponsible," "Black men ain't shit," are commonly reinforced in the rearing of black girls.

From my childhood I can recall many instances when black men were maligned. In fact, my first feelings of separation from my female playmates arose from comments about the character of black men. The ridicule and disdain came from a variety of sources (for example, friends, family, community role models). Few black men (save some preachers) were immune to these detractions.

The strength of these myths has been very powerful in black communities. So powerful, in fact, that when many black women encounter men who do not fit the stereotypes, their reaction is one of suspicion. Incredulously, they ask: "What's this brother's game? Why is he trying to hide the way we know he really is? That nigger is just trying to get over." Rather than embracing and reinforcing positive behavior, they reject his uprightness and mock his sincerity.

Almost universally, black boys, then men, are obliquely treated as helpless children by black women. Black women may believe they are being supportive but are, in actuality, insulting and disparaging. Black males are second-guessed, infantilized, and patronized. Their women (mothers, sisters, wives) assume they are unable to understand the complexities of the world and are poised and trained to protect them from their simple-mindedness and from their social and economic ineptitude.

Scene: EVENING MEETING AT THE LOCAL MENTAL HEALTH
AGENCY. THE PANEL ON THE EDUCATION AND DEVELOPMENT
OF CHILDREN IS ABOUT TO END

DR. DAVISON: . . . and so the education of children will be
very important.

BLACK FEMALE INTERLOPER [*rises and interrupts*]: What Dr.
Davison is saying is that . . .

[*Later in private conversation with this interloper*]

DR. DAVISON [*sarcastically*]: Was I speaking a language commonly unspoken here? I thought I was perfectly clear in
my statements.

BLACK FEMALE INTERLOPER: Well, I was just explaining to the
people that—

DR. DAVISON [*interrupting and impatient*]: Why do you feel
that you need to explain or interpret what I say?

BLACK FEMALE INTERLOPER [*defiantly*]: I was just trying to help.

DR. DAVISON: No. You were trying to mother me. I don't need
a mother. I have a mother. She's let me talk for myself for
quite a while now.

BLACK FEMALE INTERLOPER [*still defiant, but somewhat
wounded*]: I just didn't think that they understood you.

DR. DAVISON [*sticking to his guns*]: Well, then, you were
mothering them too. They're grownups. They can say
what they need to say. Take care of yourself and let us
take care of ourselves. Okay? What do you think? [*Black
female interloper angrily stalks away. Dr. Davison samples
another hors d'oeuvre*]

The portrayal of black men as irresponsible, unsophisticated, and dim-witted is an argument without historical,
cultural, or sociological foundation. Having been relegated
by force and legacy of the institution of slavery to the
position of least power, black men have been overlooked
and ignored in United States society (and I daresay by
much of the rest of the world). Many other groups have

enjoyed upward mobility while spurning the black man, sanctioning his position as societal pariah and perpetual occupant of the bottom rung. The media and transmitted social values have historically portrayed the black man as a low form of human development, a being with little cognitive ability but considerable primitive urges (for example, hedonism, violence, hypersexuality).

Virtually everyone, irrespective of ethnicity, gender, or race, endorses these myths. Whether the offending parties are white males, black females, Asian males, or whomever, there exists some collective level of disdain in reference to black males. The motivation for these detractors seems to be related to some self-serving interest; enhancement and elevation of self, rationalization and justification for treatment meted out, or simply to be fashionable and in step with their peers.

Subconsciously many people treat the adoption of this myth as a part of the socialization process. The black male of myth serves as a base to which all others may compare their attainments and social standing. Notably and regrettably, recent immigrants to the United States have attested to the strength of these myths in the character of United States society. Anxious to be "good Americans," they have learned and incorporated such ideas into their family values. As proof, one need only note the continuing and increasing rift between recent immigrants to the United States and many urban black communities.

Stereotyping and maligning black men is far too common in our society. Black men, as a group, do not act and have never acted in the fashions assumed by many persons and groups. It is myth and, as such, is specious and should be dismissed. It is wrong to assume that any large group of people may be reduced to a few social types. Accordingly, one should not lend credence to the "well-founded" phenomenon of black male irresponsibility, ineptitude, and animalism. Categorized below are the more popular myths and a discussion of their present manifestations.

Black Man as Nigger

This myth portrays black males as subhuman and worthless; incapable of concerted positive effort. One ramification is that as long as a black man is reduced to *Nigger*, the subscriber to this myth need not feel threatened by challenges from these economically, socially, and psychologically bankrupt beings. *Niggers* are impotent. This myth is often employed as a trump card by a psychologically threatened person. That is, when all other efforts to elevate oneself above a black man fail, one can always invoke the ultimate leveler; *Nigger*, to negate any threat in the mind of the subscriber.

For generations adept black men have used this myth to turn the tables on unsuspecting subscribers. By causing a subscriber to believe his assessment is accurate (through feigned obsequious behavior), a black man could move upward. His future efforts would not be obstructed by the subscriber who, mistakenly, believes the *nigger* incapable, if not laughable.

For some readers such behavior from black men may seem like Tomming.[1] However, during certain eras in United States history and in certain arenas, this was the *only* way to advance without incurring the wrath of the undeniably more powerful oppressor.

Black Man as Noble Savage

This myth is one of supposed, but nonetheless condescending, admiration. Subscribers attribute some specialness (hence, nobility) to this creature, imbuing black men with a fortitude, perseverance, and stress-management ability unattainable by "lesser" parties. The logic pro-

---

1. Tomming is an allusion to a central character in Harriet Beecher Stowe's novel *Uncle Tom's Cabin*. A person who is termed an Uncle Tom is thought to act in submissive ways toward white persons. He is seen as a groveler aspiring to please white people.

gresses like this: "You must be very strong to have gone through all the things that you have experienced. I, for one, couldn't have done it. I really admire you people for your strength and determination in the face of such overwhelming odds."

On the surface, the argument seems benign, even complimentary. After all, most people would like to be admired and perceived as special. However, there are a number of underlying snares that accompany this myth. First, it offers black men a false sense of superiority. They may come to feel strong and forthright in their "supremacy." However, the attributes of fortitude, perseverance, and stress management are not functions of an individual's specialness. Regrettably, such "enviable" attributes are by-products of years of oppression and abuse. Their conception and continued necessity should be admonished, not admired.

With consideration only of the myth's false reinforcing qualities, and not of its prices, a delusive sense of superiority might be readily grasped by chronically impotent black males. However, hidden in this myth is the suggestion, "Be satisfied with your fortitudinal superiority, but please don't challenge us for our 'petty longings' (like wealth, power, respect)." The price that these noble savages pay is to be denied access to those "petty" spheres of interaction.

Second, the logic of the noble-savage myth releases some subscribers from any moral obligation to fight racism and discrimination, or their deleterious effects. This release perhaps accounts for why the noble-savage myth is so widely and enthusiastically endorsed. By invoking this, subscribers may conclude and rationalize, "Aren't black males, after all, really better off being uninitiated social animals—savages? They don't have to be 'burdened' with the headaches of actively participating in society. They're lucky! They can live relatively simple lives—unencumbered by the stresses and strains of active participation in the society."

Last, although subscribers to this myth seemingly respect and admire the strength of black men, few of these same persons rush forth to avail themselves of these "laudable" qualities. Rather than living in black communities to become infused with nobleness, they seem satisfied and willing to be "stuck" with their "foibles" toward wealth, power, and respect.

BLACK MAN AS WARRIOR

This social type is my favorite; rife with egotism and self-delusion. Most frequently, it is proffered by writers of black rhetoric. The notion is that black men, whether aware or not, are involved in a constant struggle—a war. It is an onslaught by the system, the government, *the man*, against black men. Reportedly, one must adopt the stance of *warrior* in order to survive this war against the black man. The word *genocide* is frequently spewed from such quarters. Through knowledge of one's self and history, as well as knowledge of the enemy and his machinations, a black man can, purportedly, survive the onslaughts of the system.

Such a stance undoubtedly imbues meaning into the lives of subscribers to this myth. They can concentrate on "the war" rather than on themselves and their families. Unfortunately the premise is one of conflict. And, like all warriors, they stand poised to fight even if there is no battle. Usually these *warriors* do not keep in step with changing conditions. When the time for other methods of participation becomes apparent, they are unresponsive—frozen in militarist rhetoric—left clanking their swords.

BLACK MAN AS STUD

For many years black males have been portrayed as sexual behemoths—ready at any time or any place for sexual interaction. Cast as possessing substantial and potentially uncontrollable sexual prowess, women are socialized to exercise considered judgment when engaging them at all levels. Notions about his animality; his raw, untethered sexuality; his animalistically large penis; and his richly deserved status as stud have ingrained in American culture the black man's status as sex object. Voyeuristically, people ask, "Is it true what they say about black men?"

There is an interesting analogy between the sexual harassment that women as a class have incurred and the sexual harassment that black men as a class have incurred. Just as women have complained of being treated as pairs of walking breasts, so, too, should black men complain of their treatment as pairs of walking testicles. Of course, there are black men who relish special treatment because of their purported sexual prowess. However, the acceptance of this myth ensures a reduction in humanness. Black men can be ignored (as many women are) in important spheres of interaction because their endowment is thought to be physical in nature, not mental.

Unfortunately, black men have not rushed forth to challenge or dispel this myth of black man as stud, so this culturally reinforced myth has spread largely unchecked. As black males become increasingly liberated and aware of the negative implications associated with this myth, the society will witness a backlash against this form of sexual harassment.

BLACK MAN AS CRIMINAL

This myth, which portrays black men as criminals or potential criminals, is particularly damaging. It is somewhat similar to the myth that all Italian-American men have some connection to the Mafia. However, in the case of black males, they are thought to be involved largely in petty crimes. Lest a person fall victim to the black man's criminality, he or she must be constantly vigilant to his inclination to steal, rob, mug, assault, rape, pillage, and maraud.

In certain situations, the presence of a black male constitutes "probable cause" for suspicion of criminal activity.

The black-man-as-criminal myth has contributed greatly
to our society's discriminatory practices toward black
males. For example, the relationship between law-
enforcement agencies and black males has historically
been rife with conflict. Virtually every city has experienced
significant problems in this area. Black males are often
subjected to unjustified, methodical, and routine abuse. In
fact, one of the more significant motivating factors in the
founding of the Black Panther Party for Self-Defense was
reaction to conditions that were tantamount to a police
siege upon black communities (particularly males). Some
police officers were infamous for harassing black males,
presumably as a method of discouraging their potential
criminality.

Like most black men, I have been stopped by the police
for being in the "wrong" neighborhood or for engaging in
some "suspicious" activity. I have been followed by
department-store security officers and endured inordinate
delays in the processing of banking transactions. Passersby
have held their more vulnerable loved ones closer or
clutched their bags as I approached. People (especially
women) have opted to walk the stairs rather than step into
an elevator in which this part-time psychologist, part-time
criminal, was riding.

Bad enough, you may think. But on a mundane level,
there is the equally corrosive presumption that black males
possess criminal knowledge. Strangers on the street have
asked me to steer them to a drug dealer or some other
hustler. These persons assume that black males are all
privy to nefarious activity. Although I might not be engaged
directly in actual criminal activity, I, along with all my black
male peers, am assumed to know where a person might
"score a connection."

Virtually no black male is immune to this harassment.

Most have experiences similar to mine, and it is shameful for our nation.

Relatedly, a recurrent problem for black communities is the large number of males who have been incarcerated. According to statistics compiled by the United States Department of Justice, in 1990 47 percent of jail inmates were black. This figure is staggering when one considers that black people represent 12 percent of the total United States population. Disproportionate numbers of male would-be role models have been affected by prison life and the circumstances that precipitate imprisonment.

Recently I had occasion to visit a prison. From my discussions with some of the many black men incarcerated there (as well as those who have returned to their communities), being in prison is like attending a class reunion. It was amazing how many of these men had known each other prior to imprisonment. Even I saw a few familiar faces! Brothers, cousins, fathers, nephews, and uncles.

Among the youngest prisoners, the mood seemed to be one of *passage*. For them, a prison sentence is one of the rites that is experienced on the road toward manhood. Moreover, not a few of these young men intimated that any black man who had not spent time in prison was probably a punk. Whether this attitude among the young men represented an accurate reflection of community standards or mere youthful posturing is irrelevant. That they did perceive this to be the standard is of grave significance. Obviously there must be enough models of this behavior for them to want to emulate it. If one would lend credence to the statistics, then the fact is that a significant number of potential male role models have been tainted by illicit activities and/or the perils of incarceration.

I have yet to be incarcerated, but I am fairly certain that I would rather suffer the life of a punk than enjoy the existence of a cool "street" brother. As long as some facets of black communities tie together black male identity and incarceration or criminality, then some members of those communities will continue to embrace poor role models.

These widely accepted and endorsed myths are strongly reinforced in the identity formation of black males. Inevitably, at sometime in their lives, they must contend with the prevalence of these myths, which serve to define and delimit them. For those black males who choose not to be defined by the myths, some level of incredulity and derision will follow as others attempt to confirm the myths. People will make remarks about the discrepancy between their myths and any "nontraditional" black males. (Incredibly, this is the case even as the number of "nontraditional" black males increases.)

Stagnation occurs for those black males who choose to accept and identify with the myths. Such acceptance results in social and economic self-defeat. It is death psychologically. They do not look beyond and into themselves for their own individual identity.

In many circles being "a brother" means fitting one or more of these myths. Too often, being "a brother" significantly constricts the range of individual possibility and thwarts the consideration of an existence outside the myths. Whether these myths are propagated by black males or others, our nation can ill-afford to lose still more members of such a significant segment of the population to the circumscriptions of nigger, noble savage, warrior, stud, and criminal.

10

Relationships and Mythology

lady in blue
that niggah will be back tomorrow, sayin "i'm
sorry"

lady in yellow
get this, last week my ol man came in sayin, "i
don't know how she got yr number baby, i'm
sorry"

lady in brown
no this one is it, 'o baby, ya know i waz high, i'm
sorry'

lady in purple
"i'm only human, and inadequacy is what makes
us human, & if we was perfect we wdnt have
nothin to strive for, so you might as well go on
and forgive me pretty baby, cause i'm sorry"

lady in green
"shut up bitch, i told you i waz sorry"

lady in orange
no this one is it, "i do ya like i do ya cause i thot
ya could take it, now i'm sorry"

lady in red
"now i know that ya know i love ya, but i ain't
ever gonna love ya like ya want me to love ya, i'm
sorry"

—Ntozake Shange
*For Colored Girls Who Have Considered
Suicide / When the Rainbow Is Enuf*

Stereotypes and myths affect not only how people are perceived and evaluated, but also how they interact. We often respond to individuals in accordance with the myths we believe. We expect these individuals to act consistent with our beliefs, to confirm our myths for us. Our myths are dear to us. We would not dare permit some nonconforming individual acting inconsistent with our myths to dissuade us from using them. We know at some level that our behavior and attitudes are based on myths. But, damn it, they still are *our* myths.

Scene: DINNER DATE AT AN ITALIAN RESTAURANT WITH REALLY
GOOD FETTUCINE

BOY: Honey, what's on your mind? You seem a bit preoccupied.

GIRL: I don't know. I really like you, but something's wrong.

BOY: Well, what is it? I'm not sure I even understand what you're talking about.

GIRL [*hesitantly*]: It's just that you're not at all what I'm used to. Sometimes I don't know how to deal with you.

BOY [*confused and frustrated*]: What do you mean?

GIRL: Well, you have a job, want to have children, are nice to my friends, and treat me nicely. Even those times that we've had arguments, you were supportive and understanding.

BOY: Then what the hell is the problem? Maybe I'm not understanding what you're saying, but I thought treating you with respect would be something you would like!

GIRL: It is! It just seems strange. I mean, I have to get used to it.

BOY: Well, what are you usually used to?

GIRL: Umm. I don't know. [*Pause*] You know, all my life I've been told not to trust black men. That they'll try to dog you out. But you don't seem to be that way. [*Pause*] When I talk to my girlfriends about you, they say, "That nigger's just trying to play some game." I don't know what to think.

BOY [*angry*]: So, if I was in your ass or dogging you out, then you would be happy.

GIRL: You don't have to put it *that* way. [*Pause*] But, I guess I'm more used to brothers who are like that.

BOY: You're kidding!? Well, that's stupid!

GIRL [*apprehensively*]: I just need to get use to it, baby. Why are you so angry? I'm just telling you what I feel.

BOY: Because it's bullshit! I don't have time for this kind of garbage. [*Sarcastically*] Well, when you and your girlfriends decide what you think about our relationship, let me know. [*Boy stands up and leaves restaurant*]

[*Later that evening with friends*]

GIRL [*tearful*]: . . . and then he got angry, told me I was stupid, and left the restaurant.

FRIENDS [*in chorus*]: Hey, we told you, girl. Black men ain't shit.

Black and safe relationships. A phrase I have heard repeatedly from black women is "What are you going to do for me?" Such statements have always struck me ponderously. For me, two questions always come to mind: First, "Why would you assume that you deserve to have things done for you simply because of who you are?" Until the United States moves toward a system of monarchy and divine birthrights, this question will probably remain unanswerable. My second question is "What are you going to do for yourself other than try to abuse me?" It seems that such egoistic statements are reflective of increasing self-centeredness in dyadic relationships. More likely, however, these statements represent an attitude of entitlement. Duped by the myths of strong black females and weak black males, many black women stand pedestaled, waiting for these unsubstantial men to prove themselves worthy of their mythical strength.

The form and quality of dyadic relationships for many black persons are undeniably affected by the history of their race. Disrupted kinship roles, chronic economic difficulties, racism, and discrimination have idiosyncratically affected couples who are black. Historically the institution of slavery had a particularly debilitating effect upon black couples and families. Split families, as well as slaveholders' disdain for the individual rights of black people, contributed to the dissolution and eradication of established courtship rituals. The slaveholder was motivated by financial concerns. Not unlike the machinations of today's stockbrokers, his ability to trade, buy, and sell slaves at will maximized his holdings. The courtships, marriages, and families of slaves received little respect. The relationships between black people had to remain inconsequential in order to maintain the omnipotence of the slaveholder and the slave economy. The slaveholder could control his property and keep his slaves powerless. These imposed conditions naturally resulted in disruptive relations among black people. But we've all seen *Roots*—so let's not belabor this point any further.

During later years, particularly the early and mid-1900s, relationships between black females and males again fell under strain. Large groups of black people left established homes in the rural southern United States and made new homes in the more industrialized North. Many of these people were young and sought employment, opportunity, and access to the proclaimed American system of hard work and success. Many older persons remained in the South when their children moved north. This separation of young adults from their extended families contributed to a new lack of continuity between generations.

Typically, the lives of these black immigrants were strained.[1] Not unlike their European predecessors, these people migrated to a culture distinctly different from their own. Their new environment and culture often became that of the urban ghetto.

Urban life presented unfamiliar territory in which individuals, couples, and families could succeed or fail. For many, success was realized and has been reinforced intergenerationally. Others did not achieve a better life, and their fortunes, too, have been reinforced intergenerationally. Often failure was met in the competition for jobs, as black persons vied for the same employment opportunities as other immigrants. Survival through subsistence farming was no longer available, and new economic concerns had serious effects upon families and relationships.

Things have changed drastically since the conditions that characterized the eras of enslavement and the great migration to the North. More important, not all individuals, couples, and families have responded similarly to these changes. Although social scientists would cite common circumstance, black persons have demonstrated a variety of reactions to these historical watersheds. Some have responded with resignation, some with ambitious fortitude, and some with recalcitrance. One cannot reduce the responses of millions of people to a singularity. We are all different. As families and as couples we have responded idiosyncratically to historical conditions.

Given the variety of responses that individuals may manifest, I question whether there is such an animal as *black* female/male relationships. Of course, these relationships exist in a descriptive sense. There *are* couples in which

---

1. Immigrants in the sense that they lived in many of the same places where immigrants of European extraction had settled.

both partners are black.[2] But what exactly is a *black* relationship? I am at a loss to identify factors other than ethnicity that exclusively characterize black relationships. I can think of not one factor that is common to all (or even an overwhelming majority of) black couples. Therefore, I challenge the entire range of stereotypic notions of "black" relationships. It is necessary to challenge them because all stereotypes limit the people affected by them.

These notions suggest that there exists some prescribed behavior or attitude that is manifest in *black* couples. I believe that such prescription causes many black persons to ponder what it is that they are supposed to know or have experienced that is different from the knowledge and experience of other couples. For example, what is idiosyncratic in what *black* males want from *black* females. I can think of no criterion that would serve to differentiate black males from other males.

All experiences and histories of black people are not the same. And, even if they were the same I, for one, refuse to be a slave to those experiences and histories that purportedly restrict and define me. Although black people certainly share some similarities in physical makeup (i.e., melanin), we cannot automatically assume we have all experienced oppression, prejudice, discrimination, and racism similarly. Why should we pretend that we share similar histories? We need to allow ourselves and others to vary without reprobation, and enjoy the range of relationships that all people need. Only through such allowances can people truly be free of *all* shackles, and enjoy a full life.

Unfortunately many black people go about their lives with *black* expectations. That is, they presume a similarity of behaviors, attitudes, values, and aspirations among black people. These expectations are remnants from periods when individualism on the part of black persons was im-

---

2. The warnings of alarmists notwithstanding, there are some black males still interested in black females.

possible or tantamount to suicide. In those times, sociological and economic circumstances demanded that individuals who were black band together to ensure their survival.

Although sociological and economic circumstances have changed, many persons still cling to their *black* expectations. Knowingly, they'll insist that a *brother* or *sister* should think and act in certain ways. They are likely to find people who will oblige them in their expectations. Many will be able to find the type of partner they want; one who will endeavor to meet their expectations of "blackness." Such perspectives are replete with problems, not only for ourselves, but for those we want to love. For our lovers, these *black* expectations pressure them to fit some nebulous, ill-defined, and fairly arbitrary standard, lest their "blackness" and suitability for "black" relationships be brought into question. For ourselves, we are not available for alternate, *unsanctioned* relationships that may be as pleasurable for us as our "black" ones. As well, the limitations we place on our lovers are, reciprocally, placed on us. We have little choice but to behave as *black* men and *black* women; whatever the hell that means.

I would think that most people would want to feel free to be involved with whom they desire and in ways they desire. Most people do not want to just fit some stereotypic, antediluvian idea of what others think they should be. This is particularly the case in spheres as personal as dyadic relationships. Black people need not to foist strange, capricious standards upon each other. Nor should we question the blackness of those black people who don't fit our schema. Rather, we should learn to *accommodate*.

Frightening and threatening relationships. My wife is white.[3] I'm not sure of what consequence that is, but apparently it means much to many individuals as well as to

3. If you thought "I knew it," then you need to consider the racism that resides within yourself and why. What does my statement "confirm" for you? Sounds biased to me!

the general culture. A tremendous amount of folklore exists about romantic involvement between persons from different racial groups. Arguments as varied as the violation of sexual taboos, race-mixing, treason against one's respective racial group, actions against the laws of nature, and contribution to social chaos are invoked when this subject is broached. All groups harbor some aspects of this folklore. The existence of such couples strikes at the very heart of human society, culture, and interaction; they force us to consider the notion of *us* and *them*. Such couples are perceived by many as threatening to the sense of group identity and cohesiveness. Racial purists, who come in all colors, are apt to proclaim, "We are we and they are they; black is black, and white is white; and never the twain shall meet." "After all," purists implore, "what will become of us if we 'mix' with their kind?"

The threat represented by these two-race couples is more pronounced for individuals with poor emotional and ego resources, who are particularly threatened by anything that might compromise the perceived specialness of their identified group. The threat seems to be even more profound when group membership is a function of biology (born to it) *and* is relatively unalterable (for example, race, gender).[4]

When a person has dared to look outside her or his own group for companionship, other group members must consider that either their group isn't so special (we are all human), or that the offending individual is not really part of the group (i.e., an Uncle Tom or white trash). The former consideration endorses recognition of the specialness and humanity of all people, while the latter treats others as objects and mobilizes some to "defend" their group's in-

4. Although marriage between individuals from divergent religious backgrounds is sacrilege for some groups, its practice does not evoke, from all strata of United States society, the emotional response experienced regarding marriage across racial groups.

tegrity. In most cases, however, it is less threatening to ostracize the offending group member than to question one's own tenuously held elevation above others.

In my interactions with people from different ethnic and cultural backgrounds, I have found more similarities than dissimilarities among them. Their values, beliefs, and goals are very alike. Furthermore, I can objectively report that none of the dissimilarities that exist between individuals emanate from race. Arguments suggesting that people from different racial groups are inherently different in social, intellectual, and spiritual spheres have always been used to mistreat, imprison, murder, torture, and enslave other groups—Jews in Nazi Germany, blacks in the era of slavery, and women throughout history. Why have we, as a species, not advanced beyond a level of contrived racial superiority and inferiority, beyond employing the antiquated and dysfunctional logic of racial differences? Our primordial instincts emerge like some species-specific behavior; some unalterable psychobiological reaction to those who are "different" from us. Surely, we can rise above such primitive behaviors.

I have encountered hosts of people—black, white, and otherwise—who rejected my humanness and permitted race to serve as the major criterion for interaction. However, such persons are increasingly rare in my life, as I am very selective with whom I associate. But be assured that just as I reject those white persons who would limit me, I reject those black persons who would also choose to limit me. To me it just makes good sense to refuse to be constricted in my daily interactions or in my goals by anyone, irrespective of ethnicity, color, or gender.

My spouse and I chose each other because we *love* each other. Many purportedly well-meaning persons warned us of the difficulties supposedly inherent in such a relationship. Concerns as nonsensical as "Your children won't know where they belong," "What about the race problems?" "What about the first time she calls you a nigger?"

"You have nothing in common, so you won't understand each other," "You can never go to the South," were offered as reasons for not becoming involved romantically. In my experiences most difficulties come not from *within* the couple, but from the stupidity of others' reactions *to* them. My spouse has never called me a nigger, an eventuality in such relationships, according to the soothsayers. She has, on occasion, called me a jerk or an idiot—probably a reaction to what she unreasonably considers my unreasonableness. Interestingly, many *black* people have had occasion to employ the epithet *nigger*. I've been called nigger many more times by black persons than by nonblack persons. For me, the epithet is objectionable no matter who uses it.

People have fascinating preconceptions about the character as well as the incidence of black-white couples. While teaching a course entitled Psychology of Culture, I asked students for their reactions to the following information written on the blackboard:

Dyad 1   Black Female/Black Male
Dyad 2   White Female/Black Male
Dyad 3   White Female/White Male
Dyad 4   Black Female/White Male

For Dyad 1 (Black Female/Black Male), students offered no significant information or conclusions beyond the existence of a couple who perhaps were in love.

For Dyad 2 (White Female/Black Male), students offered the following information and conclusions:

FOR HER

1. She's with him because of his sexual prowess.[5]
2. She's rebelling against her family.
3. She wants to be controlled.
4. She can't get anyone else.

5. This is the one stereotype black males have *not* hastened to decry.

5. She's a slut.
6. She's white trash.

FOR HIM

1. He's with her to obtain money.
2. He wants to be seen with a white woman.
3. He's using her for sex.
4. He wants a "freak" (sexually unrepressed person).
5. Black women are too strong for him.
6. He's an Oreo.

For Dyad 3 (White Female/White Male), students offered no significant conclusions beyond the existence of a couple who perhaps were in love.

For Dyad 4 (Black Female/White Male), students offered the following information:

FOR HER

1. She's tired of being dogged out by the brothers.
2. She wants his money.
3. She's just using him.

FOR HIM

1. He's with her because of her sexual prowess.
2. He has low self-esteem.
3. He's just sowing his wild oats.

I found the results of this exercise absolutely fascinating. Without any personal knowledge of either of the individuals who comprised the dyads, the students had little difficulty generating information for these cultural infidels. Whence comes this information? Why is it so easily called forth? How do cultural prohibitions affect an individual's likelihood to interact (on any level) with people from different racial groups? For example, if you are contemplating involvement even on a level as benign as casual conversation with someone of another race, then you may be subjecting yourself to the conclusions drawn above. Seems unlikely? Perhaps. Ask your friends.

Two instances from my personal life may serve to demonstrate further the power of these cultural stereotypes. While in graduate school, I was approached one afternoon by a contingent of black undergraduates. They came to express their concern and consternation regarding some unseemly behavior on my part, which had been witnessed by one of the students. As a graduate student, they said I was a role model for many of them, and they were concerned because I had committed the unforgivable sin; the bane of black males. I had been seen in the presence of [insert fanfare here] a white woman.

After my initial anger at their effrontery, I thought, "What white woman?" You see, their perception and tone suggested that some "white woman" and I were intimately— most probably sexually—involved. That this unknown "white woman" and I were human beings communicating with one another was inconsequential. For these students, we had been reduced to objects, the mixing of which represented significant violation of societal and cultural norms of social distance for such objects. Unabashed and with interest piqued, I asked them the particulars of the scene since it was still unfamiliar to me. Unfamiliar because I was searching my mind for this supposed liaison— as if it were any of their business.

This incident is interesting for a number of reasons. First, that these people felt so protectionistic of *the race* they were willing to suspend my individual freedom for "the good of the race." Apparently role models are to behave in ways that are deemed correct for the race. Such a perspective most assuredly has profound repercussions not only for role models, but also for their beneficiaries. Role models it seems are expected to behave *appropriately*, lest *the race* be somehow compromised. Role models must maintain constant awareness of the impact of their actions. Individual freedom and personal desires be damned. Just make certain you are representing the brothers and the sisters in exemplary fashion. Any exercise of personal freedom might besmirch the race. This seems curious to me, especially since "appropriate behavior" for black people in nontraditional endeavors is so poorly defined.

Those who assimilate role models' behaviors relinquish their responsibility for self-development. Rather than challenging themselves to venture into nontraditional spheres, they look to their role models for vicarious reinforcement. And, amazingly, they expect their role models to invariantly reflect the characteristics they envy; they must never waver from the "straight and narrow."

A second interesting aspect of this encounter was related to the students' automatic assumption that there was a sexual relationship between myself and this "white woman." This disturbed me and suggested a type of cultural reflex—that is, an unconscious and fairly invariant reaction to social stimuli. The appearance of this cultural reflex generated a number of questions for me. Why presume encounters between black males and white females must be sexual? Is this cultural taboo a remnant of the slavery era or earlier? What about love or purely business relationships? What prices for friendship do people pay whose interaction calls forth the cultural taboo? Are individuals able to enjoy other-race friendships without societal reprobations? Would a conversation between a white male and black female cause the same reactions?[6]

The second instance from my personal life occurred years later with a black female friend. Steeped in the arrogance and ignorance of the women who raised her, she hotly debated the issue of black males and white females.

She lamented the familiar but unsubstantiated story reiterated by many black women, ranting:

---

6. If you're still wondering about the status of our relationship, then your interest demonstrates the power of the cultural reflex.

Black women have it hard. There are no good black
men left. They are all snatched up. Many of the brothers are either in jail, on drugs, gay, or are total dogs.
And what burns me up more than anything is that
when you see a brother who has his act together,
who's he with?—A white girl. Even though there's a
shortage of good black men, you never see a sister
with a white man.

Undeterred, I decided to take her to task. I asked what
source she used to derive the conclusion that there exist
more examples of white female/black male couples than
black female/white male couples. And, of course, as with all
racist, sexist, or otherwise prejudiced thought, there was
no source for her data—just an overconfident and irritated
retort of "Look around!" Anticipating that response, I challenged her to support her claim through an experiment. I
proposed that during the next day we should count—
that's right, actually count—the number of such dyads.
After some hesitation, she agreed. During the next day it
became quickly apparent that the concepts of schema and
differential use of confirming and disconfirming evidence
were well at work. It seemed that my friend was suffering
from profound arithmetical and visual disabilities.

Our experiment follows:

Scene: HARRIET AND JIM SITTING ON A BENCH WATCHING PEOPLE
PASS BY

HARRIET: There's one, two examples of black men with
white women.

[*Enter white male and black female passerby*]

JIM: There's a couple you missed. You forgot to count them.
HARRIET: Oh, they look like business associates to me. You
can't really count them.
JIM: Hmm.

[*Enter black male and white female passerby*]

HARRIET: There's another. Count them. That's three, right?
JIM: Right.

> [*Enter white male and black female passerby*]

JIM: There's a black woman with a white male.
HARRIET: Looks like she's just giving him directions or some-
thing.
JIM: But they're laughing together.
HARRIET: Come on, Jim. If you're going to count every exam-
ple that you see, then what do you expect?

This was a terribly important experiment because it demonstrates the power of cognitive schema. My friend not only had difficulty recognizing the existence of black-female/white-male dyads but had fashioned ready-made (and in her mind, completely plausible) excuses or explanations of those dyads that she did see which would have disconfirmed her schema. Thus, her schema and her prejudice (". . . when you see a brother who has his act togeth-er, who's he with?—A white girl" and ". . . you never see a sister with a white man") remained intact. Even in the face of disconfirming evidence (i.e., the two couples comprised of a black female and a white male), she was, with amazing facility, able to discount this information ("Oh, they look like business associates to me. You can't really count them," and "Looks like she's just giving him directions or something"). Such cognitive machinations lie at the root of maintenance, perpetuation, and confirmation of our most dearly and fiercely held prejudices.

Moreover, in later remembrances, the disonfirming evi-dence that did exist (so paltry in the opinion of my blind, mathematically creative friend), could not be recalled at the same level as the confirming evidence.

Scene: FIVE MONTHS LATER AT A PROFESSIONAL GATHERING

JIM: Harriet, this is Barbara. I was just talking with her about our experiment. Do you remember it?

HARRIET: Yeah. You're darned right I remember it. I shut Jim
up that day. We found six or seven brothers with white
women, and not one, not even one sister with a white
man. Sisters just don't do that.
BARBARA: Yes, that's right! I was just telling him that. He just
won't accept it.
JIM: Hmm.

This issue deserves much discussion by all people since
the phenomenon of black males indiscriminately lusting
after white females is frequently offered as a truism. Socially and historically, this notion derives from the oppressive
eras during which white womanhood and black manhood
were considered opposite ends of the human sexuality
continuum. The supposed sexual delicacy and innocence
of white females had to be protected from the animalistic
sexual urges of black males. Today, especially, as black
males increasingly enter heretofore closed spheres of interaction, all people must acknowledge and address this cognitive illusion.

The argument indicting black males for their purported
uncontrollable sexual impulses toward white females is
much debated. When a black man is seen with a white
woman, anger, disgust, pity, hatred, or frustration still arise
from many quarters. Rarely is goodwill or even indifference
manifested. In some minds, the idea of sexual intercourse
between such persons is as unconscionable an act as adult
sex with children.

The black-male-lust-for-the-white-female notion is quite
powerful. It is actually a form of sexual and racial harassment perpetrated upon black males. We, who are in circles
where white females abound, are often vigilant to any inti-
mations of sexual liaison with white females. The existence
of such liaisons are often unconciously assumed by many
persons. For black males this assumption is a throwback
that conjures up the history of lynchings, burnings, and
murders related to any hint or passing thought of sex

between black males and white females. We are consequently bound from interaction by historical, cultural, and
sociological considerations. These circumstances cannot
be taken lightly or easily dismissed by black males.

Among groups of black women, the argument and its
associated prejudices are a sword of Damocles held over
the collective head of black men. It is proffered as further
evidence of the animalism of black men as well as their
irresponsibility to themselves, their women, and their communities.

For those black females who espouse such prejudices,
the argument is an excuse. It lends legitimacy to those who
choose to complain rather than to take control of their
lives. It is far easier and less threatening for them to com-
miserate with other black women about the lack of "good
black men," than to better themselves in order to attract, by
their own estimations, these reportedly rare gentlemen. Or,
alternatively, for them to have the courage to date whomever they want.

Here's some free mental-health advice for all you com-
plainers. Be healthy. Be happy. Go out with whomever you
want. Enjoy the type of relationships that you want. When
it really comes down to it, it's nobody's business except
your own. Work on self-development rather than self-
sacrifice; it's healthier. For when the time comes to die, no
one will say, "This woman gave her life and love for the
brothers and sisters, so we have another life for you to live
as your own." No! When the time comes to die, you'll be
dying. Better to have been happy with yourself and with
whomever, than to give your personal life to "the people"
while eschewing happiness for some misguided sacrifice
for "the race." To do otherwise smacks of response to
rhetoric, and I, for one, have heard enough. Let no one,
individually or collectively, white or black, abridge your
individual freedom.

If you are unattached it is because you *choose* to be
unattached. *You* choose to limit yourself to those black

men who *you* see as "good," while ignoring those black men who *are* good, but may not have a nice car, house, savings account, or fine clothes. Or you remain unattached because *you* ignore those brown, yellow, white, and red men with whom you could be happy. *You* make those choices. No one else. So, stop complaining. Don't blame anyone except yourself. It's neither black men, nor white women, nor the man in the moon. It's you!

11 ———————————————

Brother?

All for one, one for all, that is our device.
—Alexandre Dumas the Elder
The Three Musketeers

Scene: DOWNTOWN—LOOKING FOR A PLACE TO LUNCH

ARTHUR: Man, look at that brother.

FREDDIE: Where?

ARTHUR: There, on the corner, near the mailbox. [*Pause*] Nigger's clothes all torn up and shit. Looks like he ain't had a bath in two, three weeks, man. How do people let shit like that happen to them?

FREDDIE: Probably a junkie, man.

ARTHUR: No, I don't think so. He's not acting that junkie way. He just looks like he's living on the streets, man.

FREDDIE: Yeah, things are tough on brothers out there today. It's not like when we were coming up.

ARTHUR: Man, that's bullshit! The brother probably wasn't taking care of business when he was supposed to. Instead of getting an education or a trade like he had some sense, he was probably hanging out all the time or trying to get in some girl's panties, man.

FREDDIE: Yeah, but man, you gotta consider that this is the Reagan legacy! Times are tough.

ARTHUR: Man, that doesn't matter. Things have always been

tough for black men. Way before Reagan. That's a real weak excuse. People got to stop looking only at today, and plan their future by looking at the present and the past. The brother should have taken a hint from the circumstances of those around him. His father or his uncles or somebody should have tightened him up.

FREDDIE: Man, you're hard on the brother.

ARTHUR: Hey, Freddie, I'm tired of their bullshit. I had to bust my ass to get somewhere. You had to bust your ass to get where you are. Why shouldn't he have to do the same?

Sometimes when I pass black men of worsening social stature on the street, there arises a feeling of connection—an almost inexplicable affinity to these men. Inexplicable, because I know intellectually that in many spheres there lies an unbridgeable chasm between me and these men. Nonetheless there still seems to exist a curious emotional connection to these stumblers. This pestering connection is strange indeed since most of my life I have worked assiduously not to be associated with such persons. They hold too steadfast to their life circumstances. Generally I have been successful in avoiding interaction with such persons, but there still remains for me this vexing delusion that, save a few fortunate turns of fate, I could be hanging out with them. Whether their problems stem from drugs, crime, finances, undereducation, or unemployment, this enduring delusional affinity still tugs at my psyche. Damn its persistence!

I liken this strange emotional connection to delusion because it defies all manner of reason and observation. It is persistent and impervious to logic and rationality. Unmistakenly it is delusion; the case against connection is strong enough to make it laughable. They are drug addicts; I don't use drugs. They are homeless; I have a home. They hustle; I work. They are intractable louts; I am a sophisticated, urban professional. They exist; I live. Their prospects are bleak; mine are bright. I achieve; they have relented.

But still.

Where does this damnable affinity come from? Does this perception of alikeness emanate solely from my idiosyncratic thought processes? Does it come from some distant historical linkage by color? Does our nation's history exhort to me, those like me in skin color, and all observers, "They're black. And you're black. Therefore, you are brothers and sisters"?

The truth is probably some combination of all three. My own thoughts are influenced by my upbringing and have linked me to people who look like me. In weaker moments I think, "Those black men on the street probably grew up in a neighborhood very much like my own. I was just fortunate." Such thinking astonishes me because, in essence, it deemphasizes the outcome of hard work and perseverance, and highlights the uncontrollability of fortune.

Second, the common history of enslavement does tie us together in the past, but not today. This history has prompted many persons to suggest that all black people should pull together. This quaint suggestion has been a point of contention and divisiveness among black persons for many years.

Third, our nation reinforces the notion that shared oppression through discrimination, racism, and prejudice results in some sort of kinship. But I am different from others who have been similarly oppressed. Why is it so difficult at times to convince America—and myself?

This simplicity of using color to define people would be dismissed as ludicrous for white people. Imagine the reaction of all the disparate people who comprise the Caucasian race if they were unceremoniously lumped together. Relegated to the catch-all "white people," their lineages would be disregarded and ignored. Whether based on societal and historical conditions or simply never-ending romanticism, it's insulting to suggest a connection among people based on skin color.

Real or romantic, this seemingly cemented connection for black people is very powerful. Its delineation often serves as a benchmark upon which individuals base their group allegiance. Those black people who perceive the connection as real may feel obligated, at some level, to help less fortunate group members. Such helpers are likely to claim kinship with their family of "adoptive" brothers and sisters. They will endeavor to improve the emotional, financial, and social lot of their kin. And, as in many dysfunctional families, enmeshment (overinvolvement in the affairs of one's family members) is paramount. Alternatively those black persons who perceive the connection among black people as romantic may feel much less obligation to "give back to the community." These individuals will define and establish their own ethnic identity—apart from, but not unrelated to "the family." They learn to negotiate their lives with ethnic identification secondary or tertiary to their existence. They are unshackled.

It is important to protect oneself from the detrimental effects of the system at large and "the community." Both can be limiting; both can thwart personal progress and growth.

The effects of oppression, whether by the system, the self, or the culture, may be lessened by enhanced education, motivation, and peer relations. For example, a black person who is a lawyer (a fairly well-educated and motivated individual) probably does not experience as much oppression as a ghetto dweller. Although the big three are present for the lawyer, she, in all probability, is not as oppressed by her culture of origin as is the ghetto dweller. Most likely, she has learned that she is the captain of her fate. She associates with people whose perspectives are similar to her own. She is limited only by her own motivation. And she likely *did not* and *will not* permit those negative aspects of her culture of origin to dissuade her from her goals.

Many readers will interpret these writings as an endorsement of the "blaming the victim" argument; an argument that holds that the system is open and fair to everyone, and that black people need only to try harder. That is, if people do not try hard, then their problems are their own fault. Further, the argument suggests that if ghetto dwellers would only "pull themselves up by the bootstraps," then they could achieve much more. I believe that this argument is partially true. Ghetto dwellers *need* to pull themselves up by the bootstraps *because* the system is not fair and equitable. Otherwise their economic and social fates remain subject to the vicissitudes and caprices of their social system.

In the greater scheme, poverty is not the problem. I believe that the eradication of poverty is a noble, although ill-advised endeavor. For many what needs to be enriched are not pockets, but souls. All too often individuals, groups, leaders, and organizations become bogged down in the struggle to rid our nation of poverty. These do-gooders reason that everyone could succeed if only basic living needs were met. This may be credible for a small minority of folks, but surely not the majority.

For some impoverished individuals, the struggle against poverty can never be won. Some people are simply not motivated to put forth the effort necessary to extract themselves from poverty. They have accepted membership in a culture of poverty. Besides, it seems awfully naïve to believe that this nation has the ability or the motivation to eradicate poverty. People who are disquieted by the enormity of poverty might do better to work toward guaranteeing equal access to avenues of success. Through these avenues people who are *motivated* may extract themselves from the throes of poverty. To simply *give* favors to impoverished people fosters dependency.

So far this country has enjoyed a number of programs designed by politicians to address poverty: Roosevelt's New Deal, Kennedy's and Johnson's employment opportunity programs (subsumed under the Comprehensive Employment and Training Act, CETA), Johnson's unconditional War on Poverty, and Reagan's skirmish with poverty (i.e., Trickle Down Theory). Politicians can often be heard spouting noble words (particularly in election years) regarding the fight against poverty or the fight for more jobs and opportunities. But they're politicians. They're politicking.

Candidates are famous for being photographed with some individual whom they perceive to be prominent in the community from which they desire votes. Sometimes, more entertainingly, they visit neighborhoods to sample "ethnic" food. What is sad is that community members are asked to vote for someone because he looks good while eating cornbread. Voters are supposed to assume that because a candidate is pictured with Coretta, Jesse, or whomever, that she is concerned with issues pertinent to the community. What an insult. The culture-of-origin force is at work here; leveling the idiosyncrasies of black people. Rather than respecting an individual's freedom to vote according to his own needs, candidates are often foisted upon communities as "the people's choice." Those persons who dissent or do not manifest the "correct" political stance are subject to social criticism and ostracism.

All too often the vote of black people has been taken to be monolithic. The community at large has voted in the past in reaction to personalities, or tradition, or at the urging of some black "leader." Such a pattern is probably no different from the voting patterns of any other community. However, black community factions can ill-afford to vote by personality or tradition. There are just too many important issues. For so long, the black community has existed as a reliable, nonthreatening, and predictable pawn of one party. Commendably, black communities have recently demanded more power in the election process of both major political parties—and black votes are increasingly less predictable.

I believe that community factions should concentrate above all else on determining political accountability. Any politician whose election was due in part to votes from black communities must be accountable to those communities. Simply mouthing accountability when election time next comes around is insulting. If a politician ignores or placates the community for 75 percent of her term, then she should lose the next election—no matter how much cornbread she eats.

Although the numbers of ethnic-minority politicians are steadily increasing, these politicians of color must also be held accountable. To elect a black, brown, yellow, or red person is not enough. The color of a politician's skin should not be a primary, secondary, or even tertiary factor in voter preference and support. If a politician is addressing concerns that are important to you, what matter is skin color? And vice versa. It is just as disconcerting to experience insensitivity from City Hall during the administration of a black politician as during the administration of a white politician.

People who try to convince us that skin color is paramount in determining connection and allegiance to a community are either trying to dupe us or are naïve. That is far too simple an analysis. Surely we've all had occasion to be fooled by skin color. It would be unwise to assume that every politician with black skin is genuinely concerned about black communities. Similarly, it would be unwise to assume that politicians with white skin are categorically unconcerned about black communities. For example, to vote *as a black* for a Democratic candidate is simply political sloth. To vote for a black candidate because he is black ignores many pertinent political issues. It is, of course, important that black people be proportionately represented in all political arenas. However, all politicians must be held accountable. Don't let skin color fool you. Poverty and oppression are poverty and oppression, whatever their source.

Relatedly, the notion of a black community at large— singular of voice—is only a convenience that enables *all* politicians to foist their ideas upon people. I am insulted when an individual proffers himself as a representative or

voice of "the black community." It suggests the same racism for which many people castigate the "majority culture," and it restricts the range of possibilities and opinions
within a group. These "community leaders" claim to know
the black view on varied subjects. The assertion of one's
ability to represent communities implies a singularity of
beliefs, values, and goals for black communities. Not unlike
other politicians, black leaders purport to represent "the
people" or "have the people's best interests at heart." All
too often these "leaders" demonstrate that they represent
only themselves.

This observation underscores the need to choose leaders
or politicians based upon genuine interest in the variety of
community concerns, and not by skin color or political
affiliation. Blackness of skin or party affiliation are not
cartes blanches to philosophical connectedness. The days
of simply ensuring the election of a black face need to end.
A black face may not sincerely have black community interests at heart. Vote for a face that is looking out for you. The
color of that face is immaterial, as long as it is a face that is
accountable.

My God, you might even find yourself voting for a white
Republican!

12

Racists: They Come in All Colors

We must learn to live together as brothers or perish together as fools.
—Martin Luther King, Jr.

Prejudice is a raft onto which the shipwrecked mind clambers and paddles to safety.
—Ben Hecht
A Guide for the Bedevilled

I was born and reared in Philadelphia, the cradle of liberty. My childhood was not filled with glowing examples of the self-evident truths mentioned in the Declaration of Independence. Notably, while the Founding Fathers were in town some years ago authoring an exemplary and noble work, many had slaves and plantations to which they were in haste to return. The genesis of our nation is paradoxical both in thought and deed. That the United States is a racist society is an undeniable truth. But, so what?

The fact that our society is rife with racist attitudes is really of little importance. Prejudice, racism, and discrimination do exist and can have enormously debilitating effects upon people, but unless there exists a conscious and

concerted effort to address their effects, one can only bow
to their influence. Unfortunately, black people are bowed
in many ways. Black people bow to the influence of prejudice, racism, and discrimination when we decide not to
enter the work force and/or continue to seek employment.
Black people bow to their influence when we accept
chronic welfare instead of challenging ourselves to do at
least a little better than the previous generation.

We must actively fight prejudice, racism, and discrimination; we must not slacken under their influence. Moreover,
we must be *motivated* to battle their effects. However, the
level of an individual's motivation is often directly related
to one's role models and mentors. Children often rise only
to their reinforced level of expectation. Unfortunately one
may all too often witness black teenagers selling drugs to
those who would and should be their role models and
mentors. A feeling of resignation to crime, undereducation,
and street-culture values is pervasive, with many black
persons charging white society and its injustices for the
victimization of black people.

One can blame the white community, if motivated to do
so, for genocide against the black community. But this is
beside the point and smacks of worthless rhetoric. Concerns such as drug abuse, crime, gang activity, teenage
pregnancy, unemployment, underemployment, and lack of
education must be addressed by *black* communities. These
are *our* problems. They affect *us*.

I am always puzzled by people who take a posture of
entitlement, while charging white society for black problems. Such stances hinder others from striving. Perhaps
such thinking protects self-esteem by placing responsibility for one's shortcomings on others. But such thinking
endorses the view that lack of effort is acceptable since
white society *owes* black people, as a result of the effects of
slavery, prejudice, discrimination, and racism. This is non-
sense!

People, take a hint! Three hundred and fifty years of

history in these United States should have driven home the perspective of the majority culture by now. We need to reaffirm the efforts of our forebears by uplifting ourselves rather than waiting for the majority to lift us up. To wait fosters dependency, as well as resignation. How dare we resign?

Moreover, strategies of blame and charges of racism against white persons mask the nature of social exchange among different groups. As black persons are affected by racism emanating from white persons, the reverse is also stingingly true. White persons are, without doubt, subjected to black racism. They are victimized and limited by its constrictions. To believe otherwise ignores the reality of life in the United States and accords unchallenged power to the rhetoric of victims and perpetuators.

Black racism. Many people, of all skin colors and ethnicities, assert that there is no such thing as black racism. How is it possible, they would say, for people who have been victimized by racism, enslaved, oppressed, lynched, and discriminated against to be racist?[1] The suggestion of black racism seems curious and insensitive—if not immoral—when one considers that the history of the United States is replete with evidence of racism and discrimination perpetrated upon black people by white people. Even a cursory glance reveals that black people are oppressed, while white people are oppressors. However, black racism is alive and well in black communities.

To suggest that black people are victims and white people are perpetrators is far too simple an analysis of racism and its behavioral component, discrimination. Additionally it is a very time-limited perspective. Individuals who assert that black racism does not exist or that only white people

1. Amusingly black people have often been accorded free reign to abuse others in exchange for past transgressions or present injustices. A friend once remarked that when he observed some black kids harassing a white man on a subway he did nothing. He reasoned that white people deserve such treatment as a result of the past and current treatment of black people.

are capable of racism are misguided. Admittedly the last three hundred and fifty years of United States history supports the case that white racism exists. In the grand scheme of human history, three hundred and fifty years is a flash. This does not excuse the subjugation of one race by another. Rather, it is a perspective-seeking statement. Moreover, it places the responsibility to battle racism on the right persons—all of us.

Black racism, like all racism, has insidious and deleterious effects. Black people are the perpetrators of at least three distinct forms of racism.

Devaluing of the Black Race. Negative evaluations of black persons as a race by other black people is one form of racism which is manifest in black communities. There are, for example, black persons who devalue themselves and black people as a group. As zestful as other racists, they portray black persons as valueless beings. They interact in stereotypic fashion with other black persons. They question the competence of craftspeople, paraprofessionals, and professionals who are black. And they underemphasize and underestimate the accomplishments of other black persons. Statements like the following are not uncommonly heard in black communities:

> She wants to control/emasculate me like all black women do.
> The brother can't even dance.
> If you want something done right, go to the white man.
> They must have let the brother slide through school.
> The sister is just trying to get over.
> She's trying to be white.
> The company is just fronting you off.
> Black men ain't shit.

Such statements reflect the devaluation of black persons as a group. It is totally irrelevant whether the speaker is white or black. The perspective is racist.

Devaluing of colors. Another form of racism that exists in black communities is related to skin color. In other words, lightness or darkness of skin defines a part of their race consciousness. Lighter-skinned black persons have endured, in the remote and recent past, much derision and abuse from their darker-skinned brethren. Much of the chastisement has its roots in the era of slavery. Seen as less disagreeable to the sensibilities of some persons, lighter-skinned persons were sometimes afforded privileges not offered to the mass of brown and dark brown folks.[2] As a result, conflicts and difficulties arose among these groups.

Interestingly there still exists some level of animosity among members of these groups. Many brown and dark brown persons assert that preferential status still exists for lighter-skinned black persons. For example, many of my role models suggested that light-skinned blacks seemed to have more; enough to separate them from the masses. For instance, in my neighborhood, which was quite poor, there didn't seem to be many light-skinned blacks. But not too far away was Lincoln Drive, and many brown and dark brown adults insisted that Lincoln Drive was home to many light-skinned, "good-haired," "trying to be white" Negroes; "high yellows" as they were disparagingly termed. In fact, they were often called "those Lincoln Drive niggers." My neighbors seemed to hold these people in considerable disdain. As the result of skin color, light-skinned black persons were reportedly able to accomplish more than their peers. And darker-skinned persons attributed their own failure and the success of their brethren to something readily observable—skin color. Of course, as with all racist beliefs, their conclusions remained unsubstantiated.

---

2. In other circles, lightness of skin was viewed as a liability of significant consequence. Their coloring represented in many minds, the unpalatable act of race intermixture and, no doubt, resulted in considerable abuse from racial purists.

Equally tragic, darkness of skin has been a liability.
Darker-skinned persons have been objects of derision because of their color. Darker skin had been, at times, associated with all that was purportedly "low" in the Negro.
Dark-skinned persons were viewed as uneducable, igno-
rant, unsophisticated, and non-achievement-oriented, best
suited for manual labor. And although there exists no evidence to support these views, people maintained them.

This color perspective also has been adopted by black
people. Black-skinned (or, more accurately, dark-brown-
skinned) persons have been viewed negatively in segments
of black communities. Darkness of skin has come to elicit
considerable emotional response from many persons. In
fact, in some circles calling someone black (referring to
their skin color, not their ethnic-group identification) is
perceived as a disparaging remark of some significance. It
is not uncommon for children in reaction to an insult to
say, "Well, at least I'm not black." Moreover, when the
adjective *black* precedes any epithet, it connotes considerable anger and disdain; often more anger and disdain than
when the epithet is used alone. For example, when the
term *black nigger* is employed, significant trouble is likely
to ensue. However, in many situations the use of the term
nigger alone is perceived as fairly innocuous.

Incredibly, lightness and darkness of skin are still important determinants of social interaction among some black
people today.

Scene: GIRLS' LOCKER ROOM

JOYCE: I hate her.

BRENDA: Who?

JOYCE: You know who. Lisa!

BRENDA: Why? The girl seems nice to me. What did she ever
do to you?

JOYCE: She thinks she's so damned cute. Long hair, light-
skinned. Miss Thing.

BRENDA: She never seemed to be that way to me.

JOYCE: Damn, Brenda. You're so stupid sometimes. All those high yellas think they're something special. See how they all hang together. [*Pause*] And all the boys want one. They only come to see us after *Miss Cute* [*Spoken loud enough for Lisa to hear*] shoots their asses down.

[*Lisa glances over*]

[*Joyce saunters toward Lisa*]

JOYCE [*All in Lisa's face, with accompanying head, hip, torso, and hand gestures*]: You got something to say?

LISA: No. Not really.

JOYCE: That's what I thought! Yellow bitch!

Scene: TWO YOUNG WOMEN AWAITING THE ARRIVAL
OF THEIR FRIEND

RENEE: Hey, Carol. Who was that new guy I saw Diane with at the park yesterday?

CAROL: A dark-skinned brother?

RENEE: Yeah.

CAROL: Oh. His name is George.

RENEE: Does she like him?

CAROL: Yeah. She says he's all right. Treats her nice and everything. [*Pause*] But *I* could never go out with anybody like him. The nigga's so black!

[*Laughter*]

RENEE: Black?! Damn. That nigga's so black he's blue.

CAROL: How does she do it?

RENEE: I know. And when I saw them I was thinking he don't *never* need to be sitting in no sun as black as he is. Next time they go to the park they should definitely be sitting in the shade. You know what I'm saying?

CAROL: I hear you. The boy should spend the whole summer in the house.

[*Laughter*]

RENEE: With the curtains and shades closed.

[*Laughter continues*]

RENEE: Okay. Dummy up. Here she comes.

Devaluing of others. Many black persons, as venomously as other racists, hold racist views toward other groups. They are as adamant and immovable as members of other groups in their maligning of "outsiders." To suggest otherwise is pure folly, absurdity, and denial. Racism is not simply a one-sided proposition with one group as perpetrator and one as victim. Each of us, as individuals and as group members, are subject to its inequities. All of us are affected by its stereotypes. None are immune. It is part of the lens through which we see our world.

As I was growing up, the victims of black racism were Jewish persons. Vile statements against Jewish persons were rampant throughout black communities. However, there was much ambivalence around this attitude. While racist invective was hurled in the direction of Jewish persons, Jews were also seen to have positive influences in black communities. Jews offered financial and political support in helping to defend the rights of the then-less-powerful black community. There were also negative aspects of the presence of Jews in black communities. Jews purportedly owned shops and stores that charged high prices and compromised the economic stability of black communities. Together these activities (and others) contributed to a love-hate relationship between Jews and blacks.

But, as with all racist perspectives, many black persons failed to recognize the variability that comprises groups. Many of us find ourselves guilty of the same kind of racism toward Jewish persons that we decry when enacted toward us. We simply reduce them all to a singularity. They are just "those goddamned Jews," in the same fashion other groups have characterized "those goddamned niggers."

The doctrinal disparities that exist between Judaism and Christianity have long been cited as one of the underpinnings of anti-Semitism. Such religious dogma contributes greatly to anti-Semitism and becomes particularly problematic for black people since Christian churches have traditionally enjoyed a dominant (and largely unchallenged) influence in black communities. However, religious variance represents only part of the spring that allows anti-Semitism to thrive in black communities.

More recently, the manifestation of anti-Semitic attitudes and behaviors has acquired an undeniably vulgar and repugnant countenance. Dishearteningly, using Jewish persons as scapegoats has become an aspect of identity for some segments of the black community. This practice has become an accepted and approved vehicle through which the social and economic ills of some individuals and communities are externalized. Although often denied, this aspect of black community identity is pervasive enough to prompt some black "leaders" to unabashedly and viciously indict Jewish people for black community woes—past, present, and future. These "leaders," in their ignorance and with popular acquiescence, seek to lead black communities down a path of narrowness, denial, intolerance, and immorality. They seek to squash plurality and commonality under the guise of black nationalism, black unity, or black self-determination. To their own aggrandizement, they teach hate and separation, pure and simple—but destructive and inhumane.

Shamefully such black persons hoist high this banner of Jewish scapegoating, while ridiculing those black persons courageous enough to voice a dissenting humanness. Anti-Semitism cannot continue to be taught to us as children and reinforced in adulthood. Black people can no longer blithely follow preachers of hate, but must dismiss them. Their attitudes are intolerable and unpardonable, and eliminating those attitudes should be foremost on any agenda addressing race, racism, and empowerment in black communities.

Recently, people of Asian (Chinese, Vietnamese, and Korean) heritage have supplanted the Jewish owners of variety stores, pawn shops, fruit stands, grocery stores, and other small businesses in many black communities. These Asians have inherited the racist attitudes suffered by their predecessors and are now victims of black racism.

Although, like others, black people have engaged in racist behavior, traditionally they have not enjoyed the economic wherewithal necessary to engage in discriminatory practices. In order for a group to discriminate on a large scale, it must be able to exercise control of its economic fate as well as the fate of others. Black people have only begun to move toward such economic stature. However, I wouldn't look promisingly toward economic empathy from the downtrodden once they achieve their goals. History belies that. Other groups have begun poor, reaped the benefits of the American Dream, and learned to oppress those who have tried to follow them. Similarly, as black people gain strong economic footholds and become more centrally involved in business and financial communities, one can expect a concomitant amount of discrimination to come from this quarter as well. It's early! Give us time.

A strategy for lessening racism. In order to lessen racism, it should be fought on all levels and in all spheres of interaction. I believe that most people are fair-minded and think that others should be treated decently. We all want good things for ourselves and for our families. In this nation, most people are willing to defend the rights of all to enjoy the benefits of our society. It has been my experience that people from all ethnicities are eager to combat the insidious and pervasive nature of racism alongside its victims. Their zeal and dedication is courageous and admirable.

However, the spheres in which racism must be fought most vehemently are not as obvious as one might suppose. Although race hate and race supremacy groups are threatening, they are not the most dangerous and resistant spheres. Where racism exists in its *most* virulent form is in those places in which we feel most safe and comfortable:

for example, in our schools, churches, social groups, friendships, and families. Surely this must be the case, because prejudice, discrimination, and racism could not exist without some level of acquiescence or complicity from the majority of society members.

Fortunately those spheres in which racism is most unchallenged are exactly those spheres in which we as individuals are most effective, those in which we are members in good standing: our families, our peer groups, our institutions, our play groups, our work groups. Racist individuals from our respective groups will be likely to listen to us *because* we are members in good standing.

When we combat injustices (as many did in the 1950s, 1960s, and 1970s) alongside Blacks, Hispanics, gays, Native Americans, women, and others, a number of assumptions are made. First, members of our community of origin are likely to assume that our behavior is a bizarre phase. They are likely to believe that given time and maturity, we will recognize the error of our ways and discontinue our frivolous and mutinous actions. Second, other persons on our side assume our behavior reflects ulterior motives or plain nuttiness. The may come to believe that we are merely "hanging out" with some social cause. ("Slumming" was the euphemism of the 1960s and 1970s.) Skepticism regarding our sincerity and commitment is often felt. As a result, many battlers, their intentions misunderstood and unappreciated, drop the fight for justice.

The prospect of addressing racism in those groups where we are most comfortable can be frightening. Most of us flinch at the thought of becoming alienated from our social groups. For example, while black people, as a group, abhor prejudice, discrimination, and racism, we are terribly remiss in our duty to combat racism and sexism within our own communities, toward ourselves as well as toward other groups. One would think that those people who have long suffered the effects of prejudice, discrimination, and racism would be first to denounce it in *all* quarters. But this is not the case. Currently there exists significant and rampant anti-Semitism, anti-Asian (particularly Korean), and anti-gay attitudes that remain relatively unchallenged and unchecked in many black communities.

The act of considering our own groups as the battle-grounds on which social injustices are fought is quite threatening. We may find ourselves hard put to risk the censure or rebuke of our peers, families, neighbors, work associates, or institutions. Such daring represents a significant challenge to our individual socializations and may effectively compromise our ability to address affiliation needs in the comfort of the groups we know best.

When someone behaves in a discriminatory way or manifests racist attitudes, this behavior must be challenged, irrespective of that individual's ethnicity. It doesn't matter if a racist is white, black, or otherwise. Racism is racism. Racist behavior and attitudes on the part of those who are purportedly oppressed is no more palatable than when they come from those who have been traditionally cast as the oppressors. How can anyone expect racist attitudes and discriminatory behavior to cease when even the supposed victims behave as racists?

The idea that black people cannot be racist is just as untenable as the notion that all white people are racist. Many of the persons with whom I interact are, like myself, trying to be the best human beings that they can. The fact that my white friends may benefit from institutional racism while I may suffer from it is troublesome to them and to me. Such inequities must be challenged not only by the victims, but by those who are potential beneficiaries.

There is evidence that this is occurring. The face of institutional racism, commendably, is changing rapidly. People who become part of institutions are increasingly aware of built-in discriminatory practices and are endeavoring to alter them. And institutions are becoming somewhat more responsive to those ethnic people who have achieved and are qualified. Ethnic and sexual minorities are becoming part of the makeup of an increasing number of institutions. And we may expect a percentage of these folks, by virtue of their own battles with the system, to continue to fight institutional injustices.

Unfortunately, in large part, those *black* persons who are best positioned to combat institutional racism are not positively reinforced. These extremely competent and achieving individuals are seen by their racial peers as selling out or trying to be white. They are, through disparagement, driven from black communities. Although they may have been inclined to address institutionalized racism in their organizations, they quickly learn to care for themselves and not for an unappreciative and castigating group.

Imagine their frustration. In many cases, they have achieved while conquering significant personal and community obstacles. They have contended with institutional impediments to their successes. And after all these battles, their race peers indict them for "trying to be white." Such thinking is undeniably racist. The terms are nonsensical. What about one's humanness? Those persons who spew such venom and who have not heeded the signals to prepare for the future are stuck; mired in philosophies of the past. Many stand, immobile and unalterable, spouting the rhetoric of the past. Or alternatively, they flail in quixotic fashion at the windmills of genocide, the white man's plan, cultural identity, and cultural integrity.

Racism is woven into the fabric of United States society— as many have noted it is as American as apple pie. Blacks "down" and whites "up" has become so much a part of our national psyche that we are somewhat confused when such is not the case. Often misunderstood is that all United States citizens, *all of us*, are perpetrators and victims of racism. We are perpetrators when we (black or white) benefit from or hold on to ideas that castigate groups of people. We are all victimized by the limitations racism places on us in terms of social interaction, human potential, and personal growth. We are victimized by its limiting effects upon our psyches, behaviors, attitudes, and interactions.

Many of us are intimidated by the specter of racism. Its

victims and authors often feel ineffectual in battling its omnipresence. Although individuals feel overwhelmed by the enormity of racism, many strive for nonracist attitudes. Although such behavior is commendable, social-science research has suggested that attitudes remain fairly rigid once formed. This research may account for why such attitudes are particularly resistant to change and seem to manifest a recurrent significance.

The strength and persistence of racism has left many persons frustrated. Unfortunately some have used its omnipresence to their advantage; incessantly citing the obstacles to their success. Through such a practice individuals may externalize blame for their circumstances. Or, more deviously, they may obtain preferential treatment from individuals who feel guilt or shame when they consider the benefits they have reaped as a result of institutional racism.

In some circles the most damning and threatening charge one can allege is that of racism. We have become so sensitized to this charge—this racial intimidation—that the mere hint of racist allegations is enough to throw individuals and organizations into frenzied (although often misdirected) action in an effort to correct the alleged transgression (even if unfounded).

Many individuals and groups have become adept at employing strategies of racial intimidation. These people seem to threaten, "If you (white person) don't agree, comply, acquiesce to my demands or opinions, then you are racist." I think of these persons as professional ethnics—constantly lamenting the plight of black people but rarely stirring their constituents to achieve. I have even witnessed some black males use strategies of racial intimidation in their interactions with white females to further their sexual conquests. Some of these women have felt intimidated or guilty enough to go about "proving" that they are not racist. Given the right sucker, accusations of racism are drawn and cast down like a trump card overcoming cards of reason, understanding, negotiation, and sincerity.

One of my early experiences with racism occurred one afternoon on a street corner. A buddy and I, on the way home from junior high school, found ourselves awaiting a late bus. After a few minutes, a car pulled up to the corner and stopped at the light. When the white couple inside saw us, they began a furious exercise of locking their four doors. The quick twisting and turning gyrations would have made any aerobics instructor very proud. My buddy and I laughed at the idea of this couple locking their doors because two black kids were close to them. Truly, we were not at all disposed toward accosting anyone. How sad it is to judge people prior to the utterance of a word.

Sadly, when I now travel through similar neighborhoods I lock my doors!

In order to combat and address racism with some effectiveness, we must accept how our system is steeped in racism. Once we realize just how pervasive racist attitudes are, we can wisely abandon the fight to eradicate racism. Though we cannot approach eradication, we can lessen and manage it. If we accept the inevitability of racism, then we can begin to concentrate on its management, rather than on dysfunctional and ineffective eradication strategies.

All of us are racist. It is part of our upbringing as United States citizens. It is part of the rearing that motivates us to divide the world into good and bad, poor and rich, us and them. The portrayal of one group as perpetrator and another as victim truly misses the point that we must *all* strive to combat and address racism where we are most effective: in ourselves and in our social spheres.

> It is never too late to give up our
> prejudices.
> —Henry David Thoreau
> *Walden*

13

Black and White: Skin Deep or Deeper?

> . . . The color of the skin is in no way connected
> with strength of the mind or intellectual powers . . .
> —Benjamin Banneker

Rather than challenging the boundaries and limitations that race defines for us all, many people hold fast to the safety and mediocrity of time-worn approaches to race relations. Rarely do we stray from our predetermined ideas and attitudes toward members of different groups. Our approaches are, to our satisfaction, "tried and true." They guide us in our interactions with others. For most people, differences in amounts of melanin are not perceived as merely skin deep. These differences extend to other important human aspects. Melanin becomes diagnostic; black skin is equated with black values, thinking, and behavior; white skin is equated with white values, thinking, and behavior.

Actually, in a strange sort of way, these approaches follow logically. People say "After all, those folks *look* different from us, so they must *be* different from us." And, as naïvely, "These folks *look* like us, so they must *be* like us." People then go about confirming their theories of color difference:

White people have money.
Black people are potential criminals.
White people are racist.
Black people are victims of racism.
White people are good.
Black people are bad.
White people are nerds.
Black people are cool.
White people want to keep black people in their places.
Black people don't want to work for what they want.

Through the use of such approaches and theories we reinforce and retain our ideas of the "inherent" differences and problems between black and white people. Although these inherent differences and problems are highly touted, they are rarely demonstrated.

For example, at one time people assumed conflict would naturally arise in mixed-race neighborhoods, that discord and violence would reign if people tried to "mix the races." To the contrary, black people and white people have been able to live harmoniously in many different situations and for many years. When there exists an awareness of the commonality of culture and socioeconomic status, racial distinctions can be ignored. Humans, however, are generally more sensitive to dissimilarities than similarities. We are acutely aware of people who are different from us. This is particularly true when others *look* different from us. Skin color is easily identifiable and, therefore, readily assumed indicative of real differences between groups.

The utility of the color litmus test becomes apparent whenever difficulties arise between members of different racial groups. The formula allows us to assume that these difficulties are caused by inherent racial differences.

This assumption was illustrated when I had a terrible fight at recess one day with Joe, a fifth-grade classmate of mine. We were on the ground wrestling before we knew it. The teachers pulled us apart before he was able to beat the

crap out of me, and our fight became a subject of faculty
discussion. What should have been handled as two boys
being too rough on the playground turned into a micro-
cosm of racial difficulties for our nation. You see, Joe was
white.

The teachers assumed our problem was racial in nature.
In actuality we had been arguing whether Joe could have
two turns at bat when others on his team hadn't had any
turns at all. Joe was pretty good at baseball. Once I saw him
hit a ball completely over the fence without even swinging
hard. It seemed unfair that he would get two turns at bat
while the less adept (we called them "scrubs") rode the
bench. Joe was always trying to win, no matter what. A lot
of the other kids didn't like him. The point is that our fight
had nothing to do with race, but with fairness, and the
teachers didn't even try to find out what had really caused
it.

In order for us all to advance beyond the bounds of racial
distinctiveness and destiny, we must be willing to rid ourselves of our cognitive sloth. We must be willing to consider
all of the variables that differentiate people. We must also
consider everything that levels people. Every problem between persons from different racial groups is not necessarily a problem of race. Disagreement between two persons of different races may simply be a matter of opinions.
If people would venture beyond the boundaries that racism and society have defined for us, we should surely all be
enriched.

> In world history, those who have helped to build the
> same culture are not necessarily of one race, and
> those of the same race have not all participated in one
> culture. In scientific language, culture is not a func-
> tion of race.
>
> —Ruth Fulton Benedict
> *Race: Science and Politics*

In my opinion, the notion of black-white conflict is a

misperception of group membership; a cognitive misin-terpretation of reality. The term itself is a misnomer. It suggests categorizations much too large and gross to reveal anything meaningful, useful, or accurate. "Black-white con-flict" connotes significant differences between black peo-ple and white people as a function of race. In essence, that there are *black* attitudes, values, goals, and beliefs that are different from *white* attitudes, values, goals, and beliefs; that melanin differentiates us culturally. This idea is abso-lutely absurd. The presumption in itself contributes signifi-cantly to the perception of difficulties between members of each group. The notion suggests that it is quite impossible to overcome these inherent differences. After all, race (ac-cording to the notion) is biology. Black is black and white is white. They are opposites. How could anyone expect that difficulties would not exist? What absurdity! Although there may exist significant differences between people as a function of culture, such is not the case when one consid-ers race *the* distinguishing feature of culture.

One could suggest that the difference between the terms *race* and *culture*, as used commonly in our society, is a matter of semantics, or the differentiation between what is black culture and black race, or what is white culture and white race, is insignificant. But the difference between race and culture is so much more than a matter of semantics. There are people who share similarities in melanin but who do not share culture. And, conversely, there are per-sons who are quite similar culturally, who do not share skin color. Assumptions about values, attitudes, goals, and beliefs based upon categorizations as gross as race do not take into account many of the important variables—gender, economic status, educational level, religion, career type, schooling, ad infinitum—which we commonly as-sume differentiate us all.

When we discuss "white people" are we talking about persons who are Jews, Italians, upper class, lower class, Catholics? When we discuss "black people" are we talking about persons who are Catholics, Protestants, upper class, middle class, rural, Democrats, Republicans, urban? There exist myriad cultures within each of these races. I challenge anyone to identify *any* issue in which *all* black persons as a group disagree with *all* white persons as a group.

Naïvely, most of us assert that when race differences are discussed, it is usually in reference to what is considered the prototypic white person and the prototypic black person. Ah, there's the rub! Who the hell determines what is typical? This is the juncture at which misunderstanding, inaccuracies, and racism occur. What is considered average for any racial group probably varies significantly from individual to individual. Despite this lack of agreement, we sally forth armed with our misconceptions.

The notion of black-white conflict is an affectation of our general culture and reflects our use of the color litmus test. This test serves as a shorthand of sorts to decrease the amount of information we handle cognitively. By employing an "average," we need not attend to all those examples that deviate significantly from it.

In our minds, persons who "fit" our average further justify and reinforce the use of the formula. Persons who do not fit are disregarded and treated as statistical anomalies—aberrations of a sort. We are unlikely to use these "anomalies" to adjust (or challenge) our averages. With the use of this shorthand, however, we lose information and thereby increase our probability of errors when dealing with different groups. If our average remains fixed, we are likely to respond similarly to all representatives of a group, irrespective of their idiosyncracies. If we assume an unerring sameness for black people or white people, we are likely to make mistakes and miscues for the varied elements of groups. Concomitantly we will be seen as insensitive or racist.

The tenacity with which we retain our cognitive shorthand probably accounts for the plethora of books, workshops, seminars, speakers, and symposia regarding black-white race relations. That same tenacity probably accounts, too, for the failure of most of these sources to offer a definitive solution to the sometimes threatening and always bothersome problems of race relations.

As long as we view ourselves and others as members of a racial group (with common attitudes, values, goals, and beliefs), we will continue to experience failure in addressing the problem of race relations. Improved *human* relations is probably a more attainable goal.

It is racist to assume the existence of black-white race conflicts. Racist in that such an assumption, by definition, calls for a black view and a white view. That is, all differences within each group are leveled to a common *whiteness* or *blackness*. Further, the opinions of individuals from either group that do not coincide with the group average are discounted. *This* is the crux of the problem. We are all responding to an "average" with which none of us may concur.

Furthermore, it may be an average that fits none of the members of the target group. How can any idea of what is "black" or what is "white" approach accuracy in the multifaceted world of human relations? It is at best disrespectful and irresponsible. At worst, it is racist. It is impossible to derive an accurate average for the enormous range and multiplicity of opinion represented in any one group. To demonstrate, let's look at just *two* individuals from different groups.

The quality and progression of interaction between any *two* individuals is a function of many factors. Prior histories with persons from other groups, the significance both individuals attach to the interaction, the match between their cultures and subcultures, and the reinforcing nature of the interaction all contribute to the viability of the interaction. The multiplicity of these factors makes it extremely difficult to assess accurately the quality and direction of an interaction between any *two* individuals.

Now consider that there are *millions* of individuals who comprise the black race and *millions* of individuals who

comprise the white race. How can anyone, in good con-
science and with even an elementary knowledge of mathe-
matics, reduce those millions of persons to two cultural
prototypes? And, more important and telling, why would
anyone want to do so?

Nonetheless, people remain intent on the reducibility of
the multitudes. For example, students, colleagues, and
neighbors have often asked me a strangely curious and
searching question: "What is it that black people think or
feel about [a particular issue]?" Queried as if anyone, save
politicians, would be presumptuous enough to speak for
more than thirty-one million persons. In my occupational
and social communities, which are predominantly white, I
have been appointed blackologist.[1] As a psychologist who
is black, they expect me to have at my command all information pertinent to persons who are black; to possess
encyclopedic knowledge of black attitudes, black values,
black goals, and black beliefs. In many spheres, people who
find themselves the lone representative of the race are
expected to serve similar functions.

With regard to the students, colleagues, and neighbors,
it's quite interesting to note their reactions when I pose the
converse question, "What do white people think or feel
about that issue?" Puzzlement, irritation, and consternation are typical responses to my question. They seem to
wonder what motivates my query. They find it curious that
one would ask about the *white* view. Their retort is that
there is no such thing as the *white* view. "What do you
mean by the *white* view?" they ask. It seems to them that
white persons, as a group, are too wide and varied to derive
a common, singular viewpoint. There are far too many

1. Sadly, there are many persons, most notably leaders and politicians, who have based their ego enhancement and/or careers upon
acting as spokespeople. For example, in times of civil difficulty, leaders
and politicians have been infamous for emerging from their isolated
sanctuaries and proffering themselves as "voices" of the community.
There is an almost anthropological flavor to this; an expert on the
natives.

viewpoints to reduce them all to a singularity. It would be ludicrous, they assert, to think that all the different types of people, beliefs, norms, and values held by members of this group could be reduced to a single viewpoint. However, an equally ludicrous notion regarding black people seems acceptable and is rather readily furthered by both white *and* black persons in this nation. If puzzlement, irritation, and consternation are the reactions to queries about white viewpoints, shouldn't all people, irrespective of ethnicity, respond similarly when searching for *the* Asian, black, Hispanic, Native American, or white view? Aren't black people, as a group, just as varied as white people? Aren't they?

This question seems to be at the center of the matter regarding assimilation, acculturation, and individualism for black people in the United States. Many persons would assert that all black people share a common history— enslavement and oppression—that binds them as a group. As a result of this common history, there supposedly exists among black persons some commonality of viewpoints on many issues. They suggest that all black persons have common interests and perspectives that bind them together in community.

Other people would assert that personhood and individualism are paramount. They would argue that any common ties among black persons have long ago disappeared. Aligned with a philosophy of individualism and arguing that the era of slavery has ended, they would encourage each black person to forge his or her own future without concern for ancient history.

There may or may not be a shared history of slavery and oppression among all black people. However, the history of enslavement and oppression has not and does not affect all black people the same, just as the supposed advantages of being white in the general culture do not affect all white persons similarly. For example, some black persons use the history of enslavement and oppression as a motivator toward stellar achievements. They have decided not to be subject to anyone's control but their own. So they have worked hard and achieved in order to master their fates. Others use the history of enslavement and oppression as rationalization. They have decided to relent or fall victim to the supposedly indomitable effects of enslavement and oppression. Subconsciously they work just as hard to maintain a sense of victimization and abuse by the system.

The notion of a *black view*—a community view—whether forwarded by black or white people, represents a restriction of range for an entire group of people. It implies, with sophomoric simplicity, that there *is* a black view on certain subjects. Frighteningly, it is a view from which deviance by any black person brings into light his marginality, anomalousness, or "blackness." Those black persons, therefore, who do not accede to the prevalent *black* viewpoint are considered, by black and white persons, peripheral if not traitorous to the race. In white circles, the conversation goes, "Hmm. That's strange. Arthur, a friend of mine who's also black, told me something different." In black circles the conversation goes, "Nigger, you better stop tripping and get hip to what's happening. You're sounding white."

These reactions are the zenith of prejudice. Their logic reduces each individual's personhood to a groupmindedness with an acceptable, prescribed, and preapproved set or range of attitudes. Statements such as "You're different from most black people" are offered as if their utterance should be horrific; disquieting the offender to realign, straightway, with "the community." Personally, I would *hope* to be different from most people.

But let's not assume that only nonblack persons are guilty of such practices. Black people have demonstrated an adeptness at keeping other black persons in their place. We are known to berate, ostracize, and otherwise admonish individuals who do not adhere to group norms. Individualism is rarely reinforced in black communities.

It has been my experience that black individuals do not allow themselves and are not allowed by others the variations in thought, attitude, and behavior that exist for other people. It is extremely important that everyone, all of us, inspect ourselves and others for this type of restrictiveness. Limiting an individual from the exercise of his personhood and individuality through guilt, intimidation, threat of public or social censure, or discrimination should be unpalatable to everyone. And we should all, as human beings, rail against such practices.

Dishearteningly, the most racist and delimiting attitudes that I encounter consistently come from ethnic minorities. I, for example, have experienced more attempts at limitation of my behavior and attitudes by *black* people than by any other group of people. These limiters serve as "keepers of the gate," poised to rebuff any who would dare consider pursuit of goals outside its bounds. Many black persons are motivated to limit the behaviors and attitudes of those who choose individualism. They enjoin us to "Be Black," cautioning us to remain within conventional black boundaries. In order for them to maintain their perspective of the world, gatekeepers seek to abate nonconformist behaviors and attitudes.

Scene: LITTLE JAMES WALKING HOME FROM SCHOOL.

GATEKEEPER: Hey! Come here, little nigger. Where you going with them books?

JAMES: I'm on my way home from school.

GATEKEEPER: School!? Boy, ain't nobody told you yet that them books ain't going to get you nowhere.

JAMES: Huh?

GATEKEEPER: Don't "huh" me boy. [*Pause*] You might as well put them books down right now and try to get yourself a trade or something. 'Cause the white folks don't want you there, boy. I know!

   [*James hurriedly walks away*]

Some argue it is because I *am* black that these gatekeepers feel pressed to restrict me. They would suggest that the effects of slavery and oppression have significantly affected black culture and, concomitantly, the identities of black Americans. Gatekeepers may simply be reflecting the perceived need for an integrated and coherent community identity. The forays of black achievers into unusual arenas only add confusion to defining black identity for any persons they mentor.

I would argue, however, that gatekeepers, in their quest to define black identity, have forgotten that identity is not static. It changes. This is the case for both individual and community identity. Gatekeepers deny us all the right to individualism. They further the cause of group identity—groupism—in which there exists commonality of ideas, behaviors, and attitudes. This constriction of ideas, behaviors, and attitudes only serves to keep black people in their places. The only difference is that now our keepers are black.

By constricting the range of acceptable black ideas, behaviors, and attitudes, gatekeepers accentuate the supposed differences between black people and white people. They foster and maintain the separation between "them" and "us." There are many within the black community who have vested interests in perpetuating the illusion of "them and us"—perpetrator and victim. Their reasons are manifold and include:

1. *Freeing themselves from responsibility for the ills that exist in the black community.* These "victims" assert, with unshakable confidence, "It's white people who have caused the crime, lack of education, apathy, and lack of motivation in the black community."
2. *Freeing themselves from individual and personal self-determination and self-efficacy.* These "victims" assert, with relief from self-responsibility, "I could have done better except for those white people." Or more sadly, "What's the use of trying, they're just going to win anyway."

3. *Using guilt to their advantage.* These "victims" assert, with a sense of entitlement, "Your ancestors enslaved my ancestors and that's why I am unemployed/homeless/undereducated. It is now the responsibility of white society to take care of me."

These excuses are enormously detrimental to black communities.

As with racism, the "them versus us" concept eases the identification of similar and dissimilar others. People often seem motivated to identify and protect those they perceive to be part of their group. As well, they are motivated to censure those group members who dare not identify with or relent to group values. This is particularly the case when group identity and membership are reinforced by societal conditions. Deviation from group membership or group cohesion seems intolerable during times of slavery, war, economic downfall, or influx of foreigners. Dichotomies of black/white, communist/democratic, foreigner/native are most strictly held and quite powerful at these times. Those who are perceived as not part of the group are often ostracized.

In the relatively short history of the United States, blacks traditionally have been portrayed by themselves and by others as the victims of limitations with white persons as the perpetrators or delimiters. But, today, both groups are guilty of such behavior. It really doesn't matter if those who limit are white persons or black persons. Both are motivated by racism and are enforcing limitations on both groups.

I contend that *all* people in the United States are capable and culpable of racist attitudes.[2] Racism is *not* the province of any one group. To believe so is simply political expediency. Each of us, individually or as members of groups, may reflect attitudes that are racist. Racism affects and

2. Or for that matter, sexist or classist or other attitudes toward groups of people. All involve the same mechanism.

pervades us all. We are all its victims, we are all its perpetrators.

Interestingly, during times of relative social calm the
remnants of racial demarcations remain. People are slow to
change. Their cognitive sloth becomes manifest. They prefer an anesthetized existence—safe from the pain and
awareness of change. Although slavery no longer exists,
there are white people and black people who hold on to
the types of relationships that typified this era. Given the
racial prototypes of that age, as well as the racial difficulties
that persist today, one must recognize that all of us, irrespective of skin color or ethnicity, may be guilty of racism.

The sense of community for black folks has been, traditionally, an important sociological and psychological construct. At present, however, its continued dominion and
power may actually contribute to racism, to the limitations
and restrictions that we place on ourselves and others.
Although functional and essential during earlier times, its
utility in the multifaceted and pluralistic world of today is
questionable. Our sense of community may actually serve
to constrict our humanness (in the name of black identity)
and keep us entrenched in the racial demarcations of the
past.

14 ─────────────────────

Tom and Sally in the Nineties and Beyond

> Nothing will ever be attempted, if all possible objections must be first overcome.
> —Samuel Johnson

Scene: TWO BLACK PROFESSIONAL COUPLES AT THEIR WEEKLY GAME OF PINOCHLE.

ROSE: You know Karen—our housekeeper?

VERONICA: Yes.

ROSE: Last week her boy Robert was shot in a gang fight.

VERONICA: Oh no. Is he all right?

ROSE: Yes, he's going to be okay. But, Karen . . . Karen's thinking about moving her family south. But she doesn't have enough money. [*Pause*] Pete, maybe we should give her a loan or something.

NORM: I wouldn't. You'll never see your money again. Those type of people don't understand the value of money. Nothing against Karen. She seems nice, but those folks from the East Side are terrible. They don't want to work. They just want to drink, get high, fight, gamble, and have babies.

ROSE: Well, I'd like to help Karen and those other people too. It just seems no matter what you do, it's not enough. There are always more people to help.

PETE: Well, I'm not helping at all.

VERONICA: That's kind of a cold attitude. They're black, just like you.

PETE: No, that's the problem. They're not at all like me. I worked hard for everything I got.

ROSE: Oh, Lord. Now we have to hear this speech.

PETE: That's right! My granddaddy worked hard every day for what he gave to his family. And my father worked hard. Now I work hard for my family. So when my children have children they will have something to build with. If I have to work hard, so do those people. If they don't want to work, then to hell with them.

VERONICA: You sound like some white bigot.

PETE: I'm not a bigot. Just a realist. Those are the facts of life. You work for what you get. I didn't make up the rules, but I damned sure know them. They know the rules too. They just don't want to play the game.

ROSE: Sometimes, Pete, you make me so mad at you. Always forgetting where you come from.

PETE: I haven't forgot. I come from my mother and father and my family. I don't come from those folks. I don't know them, and they don't know me. And I like it fine that way.

VERONICA: But they need a hand.

PETE: A hand? You mean a handout, don't you? Well, I don't want to hear it.

Scene: TWO BLACK, POOR COUPLES AT THEIR WEEKLY GAME OF TONK.

TINA: Earl, tell Kenny and Darlene about that house you went to yesterday.

EARL: Oh yeah. I had a delivery out in the Heights, and when I got to the door, guess who answered it?—A sister.

DARLENE: Is that right? I thought everything over there was white.

EARL: So did I. But, this black family's living over there, big as day.

KENNY: So what happened?

EARL: I get in the house, and it was beautiful. Art and Persian rugs and a piano and all kinds of white shit.

KENNY: And niggahs owned it, huh?

EARL: Yeah. He's some kind of doctor, and I think she works in some big job at the bank.

DARLENE: Damn. It sure would be nice to have one of those big old houses.

EARL: Yeah, but they're the only spots in the neighborhood. I didn't see anybody else in the Heights who was black, unless they was the maid or the trash man.

TINA: Tell them what happened next.

EARL: Well, this lady walked over to me, wrote me a check, and said to leave. She didn't even acknowledge that I was a brother. She just handed me the check, opened the door, and walked away like I was some kind of servant.

KENNY: How you know she was being that way?

EARL: Hey, man. I knew. I was there, not you. Anyway, I thought about that all day and when I got home, I talked to Tina about it.

DARLENE: What did you think, Earl?

EARL: I don't know. It just bothered me that those folks— black just like you and me—lived there in the Heights in that big, pretty house, and the rest of us have to live here.

DARLENE: Well, I'm sure they worked hard for what they got.

EARL: I bet they did, too. But that still don't excuse them for being like they're better than everybody. I hate that.

KENNY: Yeah, I know what you mean. This sister at work got some piece of promotion, and started treating me like garbage in the rain. Now she hangs with the white folks. Now she be eating corned beef sandwiches when before she was sucking on chicken wings just like the rest of us.

EARL: Niggahs is something else when they get big. Start

acting white, sounding white, being white. And then they dog us poor people out.

TINA: I kinda feel sorry for them bourgeois black people. You know that white folks ain't never gonna accept them. And those black people ain't never gonna want to be part of us. They must be kinda lonely.

KENNY: Well, who cares? That's what they get for trying to be white. Shit. We got to struggle everyday for what we get. They just get it handed to them. They got their education and degrees and all that, but as far as I'm concerned, they'll never be brothers and sisters.

At one time the ideology that *none of us are free until all of us are free* was a watchword in the struggle for civil rights that helped to tie us all together as a family and as a *community*. However, the concept of "the black community" has evolved an essence in and of itself, too often overshadowing many of the folk who comprise the community. Through narrowness of thought, the black community reproaches those members who dare stray from its ideological clutches.

The none-or-all ideology of freedom was valuable when black people were enslaved. However, since emancipation, this notion has increasingly lost its meaning and become dated. More appropriate to today's social and economic conditions is the idea that *none of us are free until we allow each of us the freedom to become*. Free to conjoin, free to deviate. A people can be free under no lesser circumstance.

An example of the use of dated ideology is the belief that black persons who do not live within the confines of an area with a large black population or who do not share an economic status comparable to the majority of its inhabitants are not part of the community. This terribly racist notion is a dangerous parallel to the reported dissension between field niggers and house niggers during the era of slavery. It limits membership in good standing to arbitrary criteria that contribute to the circumscriptions that abound in many segments of black communities.

These arbitrary demarcations of community have led to confusion, insularism, and censure as the rest of the world becomes increasingly pluralistic. The notion of a strong, tight-knit community whose members are connected was, at one time, functional for black people, but now serves to hamstring us as a group and as individuals. Nevertheless many individuals, particularly those blacks who are upwardly mobile, feel put upon to address a perceived need to connect.

What to do?

Many persons decide to remain a part of "the community." They opt to live among its inhabitants and partake of its offerings. Others choose to live away from the community, avoiding its offerings, but remaining "connected" through charitable work or occasional social forays. Still others opt to remain as far away, in mind and body, as possible. Virtually all upwardly mobile black persons will struggle with these difficult circumstances and have to reconcile any internal discord, but the criteria for membership in good standing remains ill-considered.

For me, the connection seems to wax and wane. At times I feel particularly akin to those with less educational and economic solvency while at other times I feel nothing but indifference. The latter state becomes evident after observing too many who need help and too many who unknowingly resist assistance. Mastery of this ebb and flow of perceived connectedness represents an important psychosocial goal to be achieved by upwardly mobile black persons.

And so it goes in black communities. How to offer help without fostering dependency? How to solicit help without incurring feelings of humiliation? How to be connected without being dragged down? How to climb out with few visible role models? How to integrate successfully into the pluralistic world? How to maintain one's blackness? How not to act like those street niggers? How not to act like those bourgeois niggers?

The psychology of group membership suggests that when individuals identify or connect with a particular group, they are likely to protect and aid its members. A certain ego identification evolves for virtually all group members. The best that is represented in the group vicariously becomes part of us as individuals. The worst, too, becomes part of us as individuals. Although we differentially attend to the best and the worst—celebrating the former, chastising the latter—both are aspects of an *associative ego* for each of us.

This associative ego operates differently for those groups to which we are born and for those to which we aspire. For those groups we join, our associative egos, although connected, are not cemented, and can with relative ease be detached. We need simply renounce our association or membership to the group. Without our own disclosure, no one need ever know we were ever connected to the group. However, in the case of those groups in which membership is determined by biology (for example, race, gender), the associative ego likely becomes fully integrated with group life. The group predates (and will post-date) us, and we are reared in its norms and values. Simply through birth one gains membership—no initiation, rites of passage, or duties to perform. Connected by biology, we cannot easily divorce our group members. Our own membership as well as that of others are thrust upon us. And, similarly, the triumphs and defeats of prominent group members are thrust upon us. For example, the appointment of Thurgood Marshall to the United States Supreme Court was a prideful moment for black people and no doubt enhanced their associative egos. Alternatively, the suspicion of Wayne Williams for the murder of twenty-eight children (and his eventual conviction for the murder of two) near and in Atlanta between 1979 and 1981 was a shameful moment for black people and no doubt diminished their associative egos.

Manifest for many black persons are feelings of elation or sadness at the actions of group members. These group members are, in our own estimations, extensions of ourselves. We become either bolstered by or saddled with the actions of group members. So connected are we to these persons that we know them, familially, as Michael, Jesse, Coretta, Bill, Diana, Clarence. It would seem that we are connected—yoked by race—to such persons and their deeds.

But is this always the case? Are there times when identified birth group is inconsequential or even changeable? One would think not. Even persons from disparate and discordant groups agree upon the criterion for membership. No one—member or not—is allowed to change affiliation. For example, not only do black persons instruct us that we are "black," but white persons also instruct us that we are "black." We are not allowed to entertain "whiteness" or even neutrality. Imagine the turmoil, chaos, and anger if a group of prominent black persons announced on television that from this day forward they would like to be considered white or colorless. Some people would respond with bemusement, some with irritation and derision. Such an announcement would upset us and our perception of the world—the social (and racial) order. Everyone seems to concur in our race-conscious society: "Black is black and white is white, and pity the dolt who would claim otherwise."

So predominant is our racial order that there exists no margin for race-group membership. Sadly we all have been schooled in the narrowness necessary to maintain the racial order. Any doubts?

A short exam appears below. Let's see how well we all do.

RACE CONSCIOUSNESS TEST
FOR UNITED STATES CITIZENS

Scenario: A child is born to parents who come from disparate racial backgrounds.

Instructions: For each set of parents, determine the race of their offspring.

What race is a child born to a:

		Child's race
1.	BLACK father and a GREEK mother?	_____
2.	BLACK father and a CHICANO mother?	_____
3.	BLACK father and a WHITE JEWISH mother?	_____
4.	BLACK father and a BLACK mother?	_____
5.	BLACK father and a JAPANESE mother?	_____
6.	BLACK father and a ITALIAN mother?	_____
7.	BLACK father and a NAVAJO mother?	_____
8.	BLACK father and a PUERTO RICAN mother?	_____

If you answered BLACK to more than one question above, then the power of the racial order is demonstrated. For a significant portion of the United States population, many if not all of the children above would be classified as black. The prevalent belief is that if a black person has contributed to one's gene pool, then one is black.

Langston Hughes, in his book *Simple Takes a Wife*, skillfully captures what was then and in many circles still is the tenor of race consciousness in the United States. He writes: "Negro blood is sure powerful—because just *one* drop of black blood makes a colored man. *One* drop—you are a Negro! . . . Black is powerful."

I am certain that a portion of respondents did not answer that all the children were black. Segments of our society have become more accepting of differences between people and less dependent upon labeling. Recently, many of the fathers and mothers listed above have acquired the title *people of color*. Therefore, as nebulous as the term, their children would be children of color. Perhaps this catch-all is a better alternative than reference to each separate group—that has yet to be determined. However, it is possible that some persons would use this nonspecific reference to describe all offspring above. Interestingly, even with our new-found sophistication, we still maintain our race consciousness. We've just moved from white and black, white and brown, white and yellow, and white and red, to white and people of color (all others).

Just being parsimonious, I suppose.

I would be remiss if I neglected to address those persons who would question the validity of the test above based upon methodological concerns. They might argue that since all the fathers in the test were black, some respondents would see blackness as a critical determinant. That somehow the racial background of the father is more heavily weighted than the racial background of the mother. I believe that such arguments are not only racist, but sexist. With sexism, the notion that the male is a more influential determinant of the child's race simply reflects long-standing societal values about the relative importance of partners in relationships. As regards racism, the argument alludes to the theory that once black male blood—even a drop as Hughes suggests—has dirtied your genetic make-up, you are irrevocably sullied. And, further, no amount of "other" blood could possibly *cleanse* you.

To address the possibility that the father's background is the major determinant of the child's race, let's take another test.

RACE CONSCIOUSNESS TEST
FOR UNITED STATES CITIZENS
(REVISED)

Scenario: A child is born to parents who come from disparate racial backgrounds.

Instructions: For each set of parents, determine the race of their offspring.

What race is a child born to a:

		Child's race
1.	WHITE father and a CHICANO mother?	_____
2.	WHITE father and a BLACK mother?	_____
3.	WHITE father and a JAPANESE mother?	_____
4.	WHITE father and a NAVAJO mother?	_____
5.	WHITE father and a PUERTO RICAN mother?	_____

Were you able to answer WHITE to any of the questions? If not, then perhaps every person of color's blood is powerful. It is not the father's racial background, but the person of color's background that seems influential in determining the color scheme. The purity of the white race versus the differential "sullying" effects of other races is at the heart of our responses.

So you come across a person who has a black father and a white mother; the offspring insists that she is white. What do you think?

Thus, unclear racial lines may contribute to individuals not quite fitting into the preconceived social order. So, too, may the effects of education, training, and child-rearing philosophies affect the *fit* between the individual and the social order. For example, individuals may presume that black males are undereducated and unsophisticated. However, there are myriad instances in which this is not the case. When we fit the perceived social order by remaining uneducated and unsophisticated, we contribute to the proliferation of racist perspectives. When we do not fit the perceived social order, then we challenge its accuracy and utility.

On not quite fitting in. For an individual born in an area of the United States with a large black population to become successful, she will most likely experience some marginality or lack of connectedness to the pluralistic world and, as well, to the black community. She will not be fully accepted in the pluralistic society, and will be circumspective of full acceptance from her original community. For her there will be, at some level, a rejection of her ascribed cultural status and an overture, at the very least, toward an achieved cultural status. She will find it very difficult to maintain her relationships with her childhood friends and, at the same time, develop business relationships.

For instance, she may become an engineer, but will likely find it difficult to maintain her ascribed status in the black community. Yes, she can associate with her childhood friends, or actually live in her old neighborhood, but she will not quite fit in. It will be difficult for her to "hang" with her homegirls. She may instead choose to live in a community consistent with her achieved status. But she will not quite fit in there either. Some people will be reluctant to accept her in this new community. This is marginality; not quite fitting in anywhere.

Marginal persons exist in a sort of societal limbo. These social misfits, if you will, do not easily find harbor with black or white groups. Some withdraw socially from both groups, preferring minimal interaction with people and the retreat of home. Others rectify the lack of social fit by identifying with neither group. They prefer to seek out others who will join them in the freedom of creating their own culture, their own social niches. Still others become truly multicultural. They travel easily from culture to culture; adjusting, acclimating, fitting in anywhere, but belonging nowhere.

Black people who are professionals often find themselves in such curious positions. As with all professionals, they have worked diligently and assiduously *to become*. However, the discrimination that the engineer described above will be subjected to throughout her life sets her apart from the peer group in which she was born (ascribed) as well as from those in the peer group to which she has risen (achieved). She may find herself battling discrimination, racism, and sexism on two fronts: in white communities and in black communities. To compound the intensity of her fight, she may also be battling her own self-defeating thoughts.

Let's take the example of Barbara, a college student.

Barbara grew up in East St. Louis with her brothers and sisters. Mom and Dad never seemed to have very much to give her except love and encouragement. Barbara had some friends when she was young, but as her interests turned toward her future, and less toward boys, their friendships weakened. To fill the time previously spent with her friends, Barbara found herself increasingly involved in her schoolwork.

In college, Barbara became involved with new friends who supported her goals. This was important for her since at home no one seemed to even understand her goals, let alone support them. Interestingly, some of her new friends were white, Hispanic, and Asian. Interaction with people from different ethnic backgrounds was uncharted territory for Barbara and ran counter to the admonitions of much of her community. Over the years black people had often advised her never to trust white people. She found that not all white people were bad.

Barbara was always glad to get some time off and would return home during semester breaks. Being away at school and not around many black persons, she felt a need to become "rooted" again in the black community. However, she soon discovered on her visits home that she didn't quite fit in. She felt *different* from her old friends and was afraid that she was growing too fast and too far away from "the community." At the same time, Barbara felt that her new friends were incapable of being supportive and understanding of her history and background as a black woman. She considered quitting school or transferring to the local college, but after a discussion with her parents she attributed that consideration to homesickness.

Her old friends were still just "hanging out," and as far as she could see no real improvement was in sight for their dysfunctional behavior. They seemed stuck in their life situations and *unwilling* to break free. Two were actually pregnant! Barbara's friends teased her about the "new and strange" way she acted. They said, "You'd better stop hanging with those white folks. You're starting to sound and act like them."

She returned to college somewhat confused, but resolute to maintain her roots, although this strategy made little sense for her. She felt she should be able to "be black," while still meeting other types of people. She soon began interacting with her new friends and peers at school.

Barbara knew that soon she would have to make some important decisions about herself and her connection to the black community. She knew that, in general, the black community is recalcitrant in accepting those who do not follow the party line; that there are significant prices people pay to be "individuals." But for her the party line had never seemed clearly set. At different times "being black" had meant anything from promoting pan-Africanism to being antiwhite.

Barbara became concerned about how she would be perceived in the community. Success in the pluralistic world, to many people, meant "selling out." She thought that people were being too literal about this black/white thing. The opposing nature of black and white in the world of color should not translate to opposition in human interaction. Besides, she had always felt more free just being herself.

As her education continued, Barbara found that there were decent (as well as indecent) people in all groups. Race or gender did not categorically define philosophical kindredness. Barbara's new perspective of judging individuals by their character and not by melanin or genitalia began to spread to other aspects of her life. She found it increasingly difficult to make generalizations for any group of people, and found herself uncomfortable around those who did. Her development continued, to the disquietude of her community of origin. It all made sense to her if she was to develop to her fullest potential, if she was *to become*. So, she thought, to hell with them.

Unfortunately, for many upwardly mobile black persons, distancing at some level between themselves and "the community" is necessary *to become*. This often results in estrangement between both parties. If this practice continues, the nation will experience an increasing rift between black, middle-class, upwardly mobile persons and the supposed "masses." Urban areas will continue to experience growth of an underclass of folks who will perpetuate the cycle of poverty. Although the sense of community was, at one time, quite important in the survival and development of black people, there are now aspects of that sensibility that serve to impede individual growth. We must move away from those myths that restrict our development. We must allow each of us to be free. Race consciousness and separation must decrease as we explore our humanness in a pluralistic world. Without the removal of these community obstacles, many black individuals will continue to remain immobile as the parade toward pluralism marches on. Black persons who *become* will live increasingly in neighborhoods that are racially and ethnically braided. Their children will develop in these neighborhoods and learn to attend less to black separatism and more to human connectedness.

15 _____

Man, Get That Comb Out of Your Hair: Roads to Inclusion

> Of my two "handicaps," being female put many more obstacles in my path than being black.
> —Shirley Chisholm

The title above has both literal and figurative connotations. The literal practice of wearing combs, plastic bags, or a "do rag" in one's hair begs attention from this author. It is unsightly and, regrettably, brings to mind the stereotypic image of black males perpetuated by media and popular culture. It's reminiscent of Buckwheat, that lovable character from the "Our Gang" comedies who invariably and unmistakenly was in need of having his hair combed. It makes black men into clowns—irreverent and disrespectful of self and others.

I understand the figurative message. These practices are signs of independence and nonadherence to conventions that many see as "white." The argument: "What matter is this comb in my hair? It's my skin color that is the variable with which the society is concerned. I could comb my hair, brush my teeth, wash my body, wear a tuxedo, and speak the King's English. Still it wouldn't matter toward employment, recognition of my humanity, or in gaining respect from others."

This argument is credible, but only in very limited spheres. We have to be aggressive in our movement upward *and* outward. Not aggressive in terms of violence or intimidation, but in terms of stating, verbally and nonverbally, who we are. By presenting challenges in education, social interactions, employment, aspirations, and values, *the system must* respond. It must give credence and respect to those persons who demonstrate the social, emotional, and professional wherewithal to compete effectively within *its* realms.

Let's look at an example of a person who compromises his ability to compete. A man once presented himself to me for a job interview. He appeared relieved that a black man would be the interviewer. He had no résumé, no command of his native language, wore dirty jeans, and exhibited an attitude of entitlement. His work history was sketchy and his training was negligible. He ended his interview with, "Come on, bro. I really needs this gig. How you gonna play me? Not like a dope fiend, I hope." I would argue that this individual was not presenting a challenge to the system. He was ill-prepared to compete in the system. He was, in essence, "playing" himself.

We must get these combs out of our hair. By not presenting challenges to the structure and psyche of organizations, and to United States society in general, the system can remain relatively unresponsive. To remove oneself from competition through some mistaken ideological protest or identification with some antiquated perspective only serves to reinforce the system that discriminates against you. We can effectively be ignored, with our views, attitudes, and opinions treated as inconsequential to *important* spheres of interaction. Despite past histories and experiences, one must continue to strive and achieve in *this* society. Because when all is said and done, we still reside in the United States of America. This is our nation too. Become part of it. Don't be invisible.[1]

The way to achievement is clearly set. There may be significant obstacles or we may not like the road that we must travel, but the road *is* there. However, you must first get *on* the road in order to reach your destination. One must seriously consider whether a revolutionary bent, or standing on the corner, or hanging out with the fellas, or individual nonadherence to conventionality, or other similar rebellion puts one on the road. If it doesn't, decide if you want to be on the road.

If you choose to be on the road, search out others who have made a similar decision, and give each other emotional and social support. Establish norms, beliefs, and values in response to your mutual needs. Avoid misguided and ill-conceived notions of what others similar to you in skin color, but not in philosophical outlook, deem appropriate. If, however, you choose not to be on the road, then shut up, stop complaining, and don't block the intersection for those of us who decide to travel the road. You have made your choice. The contingencies are there. It's just a matter of what you decide for your life.

Some sights along the road. A case in point comes from my own life experiences. I am aware of a man who has been hanging out on the same street corner for more than twenty-five years. He was there during my early adolescence and possibly prior to that time. He was there each day as I walked home from high school and when I came home during breaks from college. He was there the last time I visited home and is probably there today. Sadly, one can find such individuals in any large urban ghetto. I would think that part of the reason he's there relates to habit. Hanging out on the corner has become part of his daily ritualized behavior. However, a large part must be

---

1. The state of being invisible is an allusion to Ralph Ellison's book *Invisible Man*.

related to the few social structures through which he might have basic psychological needs met.

We all have these needs; those needs that help most of us live relatively sane and effective lives. Among these are self-esteem, affiliation, and identity needs. Although many people would not approve of the social structures—violent gangs, criminal organizations, drug consortia—through which some black people meet these needs, they are nonetheless met.

For instance, a gang member may address self-esteem, affiliation, and identity concerns through his association with the gang. As he progresses through the hierarchy of the gang he may have self-esteem needs met that are related to his upward mobility. Friendships will be fostered that address affiliative concerns. Together these behaviors will lend the gang member a sense of identity.

But each of us have to decide if we want our needs met in ways that are dysfunctional in the long term. Or, instead, to get on the road.

Scene: RESTING AFTER A BASKETBALL PICK-UP GAME

CRAIG: How you doing, man?

WILLIE: All right.

CRAIG: Hey, I'm new in town and I'm having trouble finding out where the black folks are.

WILLIE: Well, it depends what you're looking for, man. A lot of folks go to Ebenezer Church up on the hill. That's where most of the brothers and sisters go. But, be ready for a fashion show, man.

CRAIG: Well, I'm not really a big churchgoer. Where else do people hang?

WILLIE: You don't go to church, man?! [*Pause*] Well, there's a club uptown where folks go on the weekend to dance. But sometimes the niggahs get crazy—fighting and stabbing and shit.

CRAIG [*Disillusioned*]: Okay. Well, I'll just keep trying. I was

really looking for something in the middle. Thanks anyway, man.

During my youth there seemed to exist in my community of origin a polarity—street and church. Ostensibly bad
and good. Not much from which to choose, huh? However,
through either of these social vehicles, esteem, affiliation,
and identity needs could be met. Feeling able to live in the
middle, I opted not to choose, avoiding both the street and
the church. Both, in my estimation, had aspects to avoid.
It's true that I had friends in both spheres. I mean, I wasn't
prejudiced. (Some of my best friends were gangsters or
churchgoers.) However, I chose to forge a life of my own.
The adherence to a life-style that was nonaligned with
either end of the street-church continuum required considerable emotional and psychological strength. As a consequence, I learned the value of speed. I talked fast (to
avoid the clutches of the heaven-bound) and ran fast (to
avoid physical encounters with the prison-bound). Whenever one chooses not to join, one is left to define oneself. I
suppose that the two crucial questions that those who
desire nonaligned life-styles must answer are, "Am I strong
enough to forge my own trail?" and "Am I willing to pay the
price for doing so?"
To be an individual with a self-determined life-style can
be threatening as far as self-esteem, affiliation, and identity
are concerned. People typically look to their social groups
for identity, sense of self, and belongingness. I can remember the early repercussions of my decision not to join
either sphere—long, solitary walks, a constricted social life,
riding the trolleys from one end of the city to the other,
reading, thinking, and reflecting.
I began to relish my solitude immensely. It was refuge
from the ever-present dysfunctional behavior around me.
There were also times when I enjoyed being with people.
They just became unimportant and inconsequential in regard to the life-style I was fashioning. My self-imposed

solitude enabled me to tolerate a paucity of positive peer relationships, while anchoring myself against a cultural vortex. I believe that considering most others as unimportant and inconsequential to my self-esteem and identity aided me in remaining unaffected by the crabbing phenomenon of my ghetto community. I was not going to permit anyone to drag me back into the basket. My dissociation was and always has been important. Even today, when I serve as a role model, it is not only as a psychologist and achiever, but also as an individual who will not accept limitations foisted upon me by anyone—white, black, or otherwise. This self-determination has helped me to reach goals and experiences seemingly beyond the ken of my community of origin.

Oreos, bananas, coconuts, apples, and other tasty items. Strategies of self-determination are not without repercussions. Not uncommonly, black people question the allegiance of group members who do not adhere to group norms. These dissenters often pay significant prices for their dissociation and nonallegiance. Many black people employ the terms *Uncle Tom*, *Miss Ann*, or *Oreo* (black on the outside and white on the inside), to describe such individuals' racial—and I suppose philosophical— orientations. I have been informed that this practice has analogues in other racial groups: *bananas* or *coconuts* for Hispanic Americans, and *apples* for Native Americans. Fascinatingly, there does not exist to my knowledge comparable terms for those white persons who choose to identify with other racial groups. Terms that may have similar connotations are *race-traitor* and *white trash*. These terms, I suppose, are like *Oreo*, *banana*, *coconut*, and *apple*—just not as colorful (pun intended). However, white individuals who employ terms such as *race traitor* and *white trash* are usually perceived as expressing opinions that would be at odds with large segments of their racial community. I do not believe such to be the case in many ethnic minority communities.

The nonallegiance of an individual to group norms seems more threatening to ethnic-minority persons as a group than to white persons as a group. Moreover, comparable terms seem not invoked when an ethnic-minority person chooses to identify with another ethnic group. What, if anything, does one term a black person who identifies with Hispanic Americans? A *chestnut*? Perhaps the lack of comparable terms among ethnic groups reflects that the culture toward which those who are black, brown, red, or yellow supposedly incline is predominated by white persons. However, in my experience, it seems that what most people lean toward is economic in nature, not racial.

Many black people, for example, are quite concerned with "white culture" having too dominant an influence on "black culture." They fear for themselves and for those black persons who, in their opinion, teeter at the precipice, about to fall into the "white world."

However, contrary to the warnings of doomsayers, culture preservationists, and culture conservationists, cultures do not exist in isolation, continually under threat of being usurped by other cultures. I daresay that even in times of conquest (e.g., Mayan, African, Roman), the conquerors were inexorably changed as a function of the influx of new cultural traditions. Cultures coexist—at times not amicably, but they do coexist. It seems to me that the pertinent question is not "Have group members been taken in or absorbed by the dominant culture?" Rather, the question is "Has the dominant culture been altered as a function of the influx of nondominant group members?" If one is objective, this latter question begs an unavoidable yes. Cultural diffusion does exist.

Additionally, in response to what is considered the dissipation of their culture, preservationists have often used the argument that nondominant cultures deserve to retain their self-determination. They argue that members of the culture should decide its direction, instead of forces from outside, which may be bent on absorption or negation of cultural differences. Further, preservation-minded persons suggest that through respect for cultural self-determination and expression, nondominant groups may maintain and perpetuate their identities.

This notion is interesting for a number of reasons. It first suggests a sort of cultural differentiation; that one may consider the separateness of cultures (for example, "black culture" separate from "white culture"). As an academic exercise, I suppose it is possible to consider these cultures separately, but not in everyday social discourse. I can think of no social phenomenon or situation that would differentiate black culture and white culture; no one thing that is exclusive to black or white people. Even the terms *black culture* and *white culture* seem curious to me. These "cultures" (to misuse the term) are intimately tied to one another.

Second, and relatedly, the notion of cultural self-determination assumes that people are able to exert control over their cultures, that they have the power to purposefully and predictably affect culture. Cultures are rarely *made*, they *evolve*. They are subject to the vicissitudes of cultural contact, the media, and a host of sociological, anthropological, and historical conditions.

Third, and ironically, those same preservationists who decry the tendency of the dominant culture to absorb and not respect cultural identity, do not afford the *same* self-determination for individuals within their own groups. For dissenters, social ostracism often results; rarely are they allowed, without condemnation, the expression of disparate opinions or life-styles.

Many individuals who are in the process of achieving find themselves acquiescing to the pronouncements (and sometimes ravings) of these preservationists, or facing censure in an atmosphere of persecution and fascism. For example, in the 1960s and 1970s, many black persons did not support the relatively narrow philosophies of the preservationists of the time (for example, the Black Panthers, Black Muslims). They chose not to embrace the strategies of their peers for challenging the dominant culture. Often these dissenters existed in silence for fear of reprisals of some sort. Many adherents of the culture-preservationist movement, then and now, vilify their peers as Oreos, bananas, coconuts, or apples. Unless these dissenting individuals succumb to the current *Zeitgeist*, they are castigated as traitors of a sort (i.e., Uncle Toms, house niggers); not to be afforded support in their endeavors.

Ravings of an Uncle Tom. When taken together, what does it really mean to be black? Really? What do we all have in common? What do we *all* do or think or feel or want? What do we all have in common? Enslavement of our ancestors? If so, that's really stretching; fishing for commonality. Slavery was an awfully long time ago, and not all black people were enslaved. And, even if we all descended from slaves, that era was so long ago that those supposedly common threads are, by now, seriously frayed and unraveled. Music? I don't think so. The range of music enjoyed by all people is quite varied. Food? Probably not. So what is it that we all have in common?

What do all white people share in common? I am unable to think of anything that ties people together in either of these groups other than race. And, if the answer to their commonality is race, then what behaviors, attitudes, or values characterize all people who are white or black? As soon as one begins to list the commonalities that tie together members of a group as a function of race, racism begins! For certainly, by listing the "commonalities," one is limiting the range of what people in a particular group may do, believe, or think.

In my estimation, there is more variability *within* each group than *between* groups. For example, without a doubt, there is more disparity between myself and a drug dealer who is black than between myself and a psychologist who is nonblack. Education, socioeconomic status, values, goals, and aspirations are much more significant variables for differentiation of people than is race. Sadly, people are misguided by the discernibility of race. Since race is so easily distinguished, we presume to extend its dissimilarities to other aspects of persons; suggesting values, goals, and aspirations purportedly idiosyncratic to race. Even the language of dissimilarity is folly; racial values, racial beliefs, racial aspirations. How nonsensical!

In many of the spheres in which I interact race is present, but not paramount. It's not that my friends, colleagues, and I don't notice race. We just make it inconsequential for our interactions. At the present stage of human development that is all that we can expect; humans will probably always be too primitive a species to completely discount race or gender.

Interestingly, people seem quite motivated to find and reinforce the differences rather than acknowledge the commonalities between individuals from different racial groups. We even limit *ourselves* thusly; touting our *blackness*, our *whiteness*, our *femaleness*, our *maleness* to the disregard of our humanness. Perhaps if we all recognize and respect the humanity of *ourselves*, it will help us to recognize and respect the humanity of *others*. At minimum, such recognition will free us from all the limitations we place on ourselves. Let's not reduce the humanity of ourselves and others to a matter of melanin or genitalia.

An individual may not be concerned, at all, with being an Oreo, banana, coconut, apple, or other tasty item. She may not be concerned with moving toward or away from *any* particular culture. Rather, she may be attempting to create her own *Weltansicht*; her own phenomenology. She may simply want to fashion her world and culture as neither black nor white, neither yellow nor white, neither red nor white, neither brown nor white, neither female nor male—just human.

For quite a while it has been time for black individuals to

integrate fully into the pluralistic world, even if their cultures of origin and the pluralistic world are not ready. Not to do so is disadvantageous to the individual, the cultures of origin, and the pluralistic world. We cannot exist separate from each other. Rather than castigating those achievers who are integrating into the pluralistic world, we should reinforce and strive to emulate these persons.

An example of the inanity of separatism in cultures is the field of black psychology. Oftentimes I am queried by some individual—white, black, otherwise—about some point of *black* psychology: the rearing of black children, black female-male relationships, black families. At times, clients decide to avail or not to avail themselves of my services in response to my being a *black* psychologist. I have *no* idea what black psychology is. Further, I challenge anyone to make a case for the separateness of this field. I was trained as a psychologist. So, I am a psychologist who is black, not a black psychologist. The latter seems limiting of me as well as of black people in general. It relegates and limits my practice and expertise to issues purportedly pertinent only to black persons. As well, it implies and denotes a normative set of "black" behaviors for black people. In my practice I have encountered many cases of neurosis as a function of individuals fretting over their discord with this supposed normative set.

Relatedly, I was once invited to attend a meeting for consultants to a mental health agency. Although my expertise at the time was adolescence, I was asked to conduct some training sessions in multicultural sensitivity, an area in which I had virtually no academic training. When I declined, I was then asked if I knew of any psychologists who could conduct training sessions regarding therapy with individuals aged fifteen to eighteen years.

It seemed to me that my education and expertise were qualified by my race. These mental health administrators seemed to suggest: "Surely this Negro knows only of Negroes and nothing else. We'll get a psychologist who is white when we want to deal with *real* psychology."[2] People need to be informed that Ph.D.'s do not come in black or white or brown or red or yellow. They also do not come in blue for boys and pink for girls. They come with hard work, intelligence, and perseverance. Let's not negate the training, education, or achievement of any person by making ethnicity or gender foremost.

2. Amazingly, psychologists and other therapists are legendary for engaging in such racist practices. Feigning cultural sensitivity, they often (as a matter of practice) refer ethnic clients to therapists who *match* the client's ethnic background. They often ignore important issues such as acculturation or even the presenting clinical problem. In knee-jerk fashion, they presume race as paramount in clients' clinical issues and, as unthinking, they presume an ethnically matched therapist to be privy to some secret (no doubt, tribal) mental-health information.

16 _____

We Must Overcome

> Our children may learn about heroes of the past.
> Our task is to make ourselves architects of the
> future.
>
> —Jomo Mzee Kenyatta

Scene: SCHOOL PTA MEETING

TEACHER: Members of the PTA. Tomorrow, February first, marks the beginning of Black History Month. During this month we will celebrate the achievements of black people in United States history. We'll read a book about Harriet Tubman and listen to Dr. Martin Luther King, Jr.'s speech. We will also have an African dance troupe at a school assembly, a soul food luncheon, and other events that honor the contributions of black people.

PARENT: Black History Month is a time when all Black Americans should be proud of the achievements and contributions of black people in American history. This is a time to remember Crispus Attucks; Harriet Tubman; Martin Luther King, Jr.; Rosa Parks; and George Washington Carver.

Not to belittle the efforts of those people who worked diligently to establish an official Black History Month, but it seems to me that black persons must be responsive to new times and demands rather than aligning with strategies that keep us cemented in the past—out of reach of the future. The time for singing songs (e.g., "We Shall Overcome") and waxing rhetorical has passed. I, for one, am sick and tired of hearing King's "I have a Dream" speech. Has nothing significant happened in the black community since his death? If there has been positive change, let's give some attention to it. If not, let's begin to attend to things that will bring it about, rather than reminiscing and wallowing in the past.

Every damned February I have to hear about these people. I find myself deluged with offerings of chicken, cornbread, and greens. I usually have to endure the readings of some poet wearing a daishiki and stuck in a time wrap. Television, typically a good source of mindless distraction, doesn't even provide asylum from this barrage: specials, Jane Pittman, *Roots*, Coretta, Harlem Renaissance, on and on. All in an effort to celebrate Black History Month.

I suppose that the creation of Black History Month seemed necessary to demonstrate that black people had, indeed, contributed to the history of the United States. Historically, the achievements of black people, whenever presented, were done so in isolation. The conditions that motivated and necessitated such omission from mainstream United States history were obvious. Simple prejudice, racism, and political wisdom dictated this significant departure from historical accuracy and objectivism.

When I was a school-age child, the achievements of black people were presented to me in laundry-list fashion— without context or meaning. Black persons were notably excluded from "important" United States history. All United States citizens learned of Washington, Lincoln, Jefferson, Al Bell, and John Adams. If the history textbooks were seen as accurate, the achievements of black persons were few indeed. And from the study of world history, one would have had to conclude (without benefit of scholarly, nonethnocentric works) that black persons had contributed very little. As a result, black educators, historians, and politicians felt compelled to make children aware of the contributions of all people—particularly those who were black. *Ergo*, Black History Month. However, I think that Black History Month has outlived its usefulness.

The field of black history is, by definition, separatist and exclusionary; no less separate and exclusive than the white history it sought to supplement. It suggests an enumeration and listing of the achievements of black people, often without historical context. We are *not* separate in United States history. Why be accorded a separate month for recognition? Black people have always been and will continue to be an *integral* part of United States and world history. So, let's talk and write about blacks in history, not black history. It's so much more than a matter of semantics.

This nation's history, textbooks notwithstanding, has never been exclusively white history. All types of people: Chinese, Iroquois, Japanese, Mexican, Cheyenne, French, German, Italian, Greek, black, and others have been integral in the history of the United States of America. Let educators and historians write books that accurately represent the history of the United States. If they do, then representativeness will emerge. Let's relish being included in the normal development and unfolding of United States history, rather than being a corollary to it.

I look forward to the day when King's birthday is a holiday as perfunctory as Presidents' Day; simply a day off and not a day charged with giving pride and meaning to so many. I hope those people who clamor and petition for recognition through the celebration of Black History Month will be able to point to the present endeavors and future aspirations of black individuals. Let's not hold on too desperately to the past for vicarious meaningfulness.

Concerned persons may help this process by supporting programs that foster independence and develop identity. Concurrently, those programs that perpetuate dependency and narrowness must be rejected. As positive programs increase in number, individuals in the process of becoming will be aided in their struggle to break free of old, dysfunctional strategies while overcoming group mandates.

Embracing inclusion while moving away from separatism will aid us in becoming part of the collage of pluralism. We will be active and integral members of the national community, rather than unknown quantities to be approached with caution. By *becoming* we will step toward a future of personal, social, and economic success. In order to grasp this future, black persons must continue to let go of the past. If we fail to do so, then black communities will always lag behind; faltering at those critical points in history when we need to seize and make opportunities. As a result, we will be unresponsive to new social and economic demands and our children will continue our legacy, generation after tragic generation.

About the Author

JAMES DAVISON, JR., Ph.D., is a licensed clinical psychologist in private practice with a specialization in self-defeating behavior and strategies. He has taught at the University of Utah, North Park College in Chicago, and Seattle University and has written for numerous academic publications. He lives in Seattle, Washington with his wife and two sons.